A PROFESSION OF FAITH

VOLUME 1

OF

FAITH

Christ, Character & Career

◆

John Bringardner & Randy Jordan, Eds.

DPI

DISCIPLESHIP
PUBLICATIONS
INTERNATIONAL

A Profession of Faith—Volume 1
© 2002 by Discipleship Publications International
2 Sterling Road, Billerica, Mass. 01862-2595

Printed in the United States of America

ISBN: 1-57782-170-X

Cover Design: Jennifer Matienzo
Interior Design: Tony Bonazzi

Contents

Foreword

Building Blocks

Russ Ewell

The most underrated component of world evangelism, as I see it, is the role of the professional. The disciple who has carved out a career in the secular workforce has a long Biblical lineage, birthed with Abraham and including such heroes as Joseph, Nehemiah, Mordecai, Daniel, the women who supported Jesus out of their own means (Luke 8:3) and Lydia. You hold in your hands a volume with the potential to revolutionize your view of the professional's value to God and to disciples around the world.

Growing up, I had never planned to go into the ministry, but had instead mapped out a course to be successful in business and parlay that into a career in politics. When I was baptized on December 5, 1980, my heart changed from politician to proclaimer, and I went on to become an evangelist. The role of evangelist or women's ministry leader is the critical role in evangelizing the world, but it cannot be successful independent of other complementary leadership roles. What I mean by this is that an evangelist is only as effective as the team that surrounds him. There is no way a person on the ministry staff can maintain perspective without having professional disciples' opinions, views and insights shaping his leadership. I feel that one of the reasons God has been able to give my wife, Gail, and me success in leading churches is because of the professional disciples who have supported us, spiritually, in our marriage and family, and financially.

There are a number of people in the kingdom hoping to be a part of the ministry staff, but it will not come to pass. Being a professional and a disciple does not mean that your contribution to the evangelization of the world is limited. It actually means that you are called to live your life in the workforce as a "profession of faith." I know for a fact that the church in Washington DC would not exist if we had not had the help of a number of authors in this volume and in the one that will soon follow it, like Randy Jordan and Vivian Rivera-Hanes. Randy Jordan and Clayton Walker were some of the mature men who helped my

8

two-month-old marriage develop and my twenty-seven-year-old immaturity turn into a maturity that God could use to lead a church. In fact, Randy and his wife, Jan, were one of a number of older families who provided wisdom and guidance to my young family to shorten the leadership learning curve and to enable us to navigate the painful trials of life. It was Archer Taliaferro, in his sixties and retired from the IRS, who helped me order my financial life and purchase my first family car. It was Allan Aubert, an engineer, who helped me understand the importance of technology for the kingdom, something that evolved into what is now the NET World Sector. I could go on and talk about the school teacher and principal, John Taliaferro, who gave that up to become an elder in the San Francisco Church of Christ and now serves as principal at the Hope Technology School. There was Rick Tittmann, a commander in the Navy who I prayed and studied with about pursuing the rank of captain, who helped me learn the power of organizational building in the kingdom—and with whom I rejoiced with when he was promoted to that position.

The role of the working professional is simply too vital to be relegated to a "thank you." Those in that group need the help found in this volume to multiply the number of disciples who take on this inspirational responsibility in the church. The kingdom will not progress without their number, and the world will remain unevangelized unless many of you reading these pages take up the mantle and continue the legacy.

❖❖❖

This first volume will do much to help you in the way that I was helped in my early days in Washington DC. It will teach you how to develop the foundation of a solid life. If you cannot develop the essential components of relationships, marriage and a personal walk that matches your Biblical convictions, then you will never be able to fulfill God's role for your life as a working professional. Turn the pages of this book as though you were getting the opportunity to have a personal appointment with these heroes of the faith whose names are too rarely mentioned on earth, but are highly esteemed in heaven. Godspeed in developing your "profession of faith."

Introduction

John Bringardner and Randy Jordan

Therefore, since we have a great high priest who has gone through the heavens, Jesus the Son of God, let us hold firmly to the *faith we profess.* For we do not have a high priest who is unable to sympathize with our weaknesses, but we have one who has been tempted in every way, just as we are—yet was without sin. Let us then *approach the throne of grace with confidence,* so that we may receive mercy and find grace to help us in our time of need.

Hebrews 4:14–16, emphasis added

The idea for this book came after conducting several spiritual seminars developed particularly for professionals from throughout the United States. During the seminars, we learned that the men and women in the room were indeed the "five talent" people that Jesus referred to in Matthew 25. We also learned that they were often underachievers in their home churches. The question that we heard repeated again and again was, "Why am I less successful spiritually than I am in my profession?" Although the Christian in the professional arena makes the same profession of faith at baptism as any other disciple of Jesus Christ, we have seen that he or she faces unique challenges in applying the principles of faith in the professional setting. In addition, the "personality" of a professional can produce challenges outside of work that hamper spiritual success. This book represents our attempt to place these challenges front and center so that the Christian professional can grow and indeed "approach the throne of grace with confidence."

We, along with the other chosen authors, have approached this assignment with a great deal of humility and honesty. We realize that we are writing about topics that for us have carried both personal victories and defeats, and we are willing to share them for the benefit of others. Our chapter authors are, without exception, distinguished professionals in their areas of expertise.

As you will see from their brief biographies, their professional credentials are impressive under any standard of review, but this is not why they have been chosen. Some authors you may have read from before, but for most, this will be their first time publishing on spiritual topics. The qualifying common denominator is that each writer has demonstrated a supreme desire to succeed professionally while maintaining a commitment to excellence in his or her spiritual walk with God. We are thankful for their willingness to share their lives with you.

This book, the first of two volumes, displays a unique combination of character and thematic studies. The first half of the book is focused on Biblical characters whose vocations parallel the professional world of today. The second half contains writings on themes that we believe are relevant to the life of every professional in the modern world. It is our desire that these books will serve as ongoing spiritual resource manuals for every Christian professional. Now, open your heart and prepare to receive the blessings from these disciples.

Part 1

Biblical Characters

John Bringardner holds a law degree from Florida State University and has been a member of the Florida bar since 1982, where he specialized in civil-trial practice. In 1987 he gave up his law career and moved his family to Boston where he and his wife, Emily, trained to be in the ministry. In 1990, John and Emily were asked to move to Bangkok, Thailand, where they planted the pillar church for southeast Asia. They led the church in Bangkok for two years and then moved to lead the church in Manila for one year. In 1993, John and his family moved to Los Angeles to help start the Media/Law World Sector. He passed the California bar in 1994 and now serves as general counsel for the International Churches of Christ and world sector administrator of the Media/Law World Sector.

John and Emily also serve as congregational deacon and deaconess for the Los Angeles International Church of Christ. John is listed in *Who's Who of American Lawyers*. He became a disciple in 1975 in Orlando, Florida. He and Emily have two sons, JT, 16, Michael, 15, and one daughter, Malee, 11.

1 Zenas

Finding Grace Through the Law

John Bringardner

The lamp burns dimly on the table, its flame flickering shadows in the cool, gentle breeze of night. Scrolls are scattered on the floor of the upper room, opened and stacked, crisscrossed upon each other like a tiny pyramid. Others lie on the table, small fragments of lace marking a place, a thought, a handy piece of rhetoric, waiting to roll into action. He paces by the window. Arms gesturing, he stops, wrestling to find the right word...then quickly, back to the table, the scrolls, the parchment, loosing the power of his pen, a fine golden quill given to him by his late father for luck. He savors the words like a fine wine, swirling them in his mouth for taste. Surely, this will work.

An appeal to the gods of reason? he mused. *How could his client have known that this troublemaker was a citizen of Rome? Of course, the magistrates would buy their way out of justice. It was the jailer's fault. He should have made proper inquiry. Perhaps the judge will have mercy, realizing that his client had already paid a heavy price. Ah, but the wine grows bitter. These words will not do.* A dull, heavy wave begins to build inside his head. His stomach turns. He knew. Deep down, he knew. Someone would have to pay. His client was the instigator. He had brought false charges against a Roman citizen. The magistrates were embarrassed and desperately needed to save face. There would be no reason. The law was powerless to save. If only...he could find a little grace.

Who knows where Zenas first met Paul? Maybe he was there when the magistrates wrongly tried Paul in Philippi. Perhaps, he posted bond for Jason in Thessalonica. Was he in the Areopagus of Athens for Paul's defense? Or did he stand before Gallio at the trial of Sosthenes in Corinth? No, we do not know where Zenas first met Paul, but we do know this: Paul and his companions certainly had no shortage of need for a lawyer!

Now this is only supposition, but I think Zenas met Paul in Ephesus. After all, we know that Zenas traveled with Apollos to Crete to deliver Paul's epistle to Titus. This means Zenas and Apollos were companions. We also know that Apollos went to Ephesus right after his conversion in Corinth. It is possible that Zenas was in the assembly during the riot in Ephesus. Perhaps Demetrius and his fellow artisans listened to the city clerk and brought charges against Alexander, who in turn hired Zenas for his defense. Then, during the long hours of preparation, Alexander convinced this pagan lawyer to come and see about these followers of "The Way." Maybe Zenas came to church, heard Apollos, that learned and passionate man, and found what he had always been looking for. Perhaps, Zenas, like me, found grace through the law!

I have been a lawyer for nearly twenty years. I have heard all the lawyer jokes, felt the scorn of society during the O. J. fiasco, and been shunned at Christmas parties as if I had some contagious disease. But, I have a confession to make: I love being a lawyer! For as long as I can remember, I always wanted to be a lawyer. I love the hard work, the preparation, and the parry and thrust of the fight. I love to match wits with quick footed adversaries, to parse logic and reason, to find a weakness and rip out the throat of ill prepared—whoops—I got a little carried away there! To me, the law is an honorable profession and as a Christian lawyer, Zenas has become my "patron saint." Let me share a little bit about this relatively obscure, but important professional.

The Bible refers to Zenas only once, but at least this is one more than most professions! (Pardon the jab.) In Titus 3:13, Paul concludes his letter to Titus with these remarks: "Do everything you can to help Zenas the lawyer and Apollos on their way and see that they have everything they need." Hidden in these words are several important qualities we need to examine.

Availability

Apparently, Zenas and Apollos delivered this letter to Titus while on a special mission for Paul. The customary nautical route would take them from Ephesus to Cnidus across the Mediterranean to the island of Crete, a tour of approximately four hundred miles. This journey was time consuming and often treacherous (see Acts 27). The point here is that Zenas, a professional, was available at Paul's beck and call.

Let's look at what Zenas had to do in order for this trip to occur. First, he had to clear his calendar, reassigning his caseload and talking to grumpy clients. Next, he had to arrange for his own family's needs while he was away. Finally, he had to charter the trip. Most likely, Zenas had to fund the trip out of his own personal resources. Think about it—why else would Paul ask a professional to accompany an evangelist for this trip?

Now ask yourself this question: What would you do if your ministry leader asked you to accompany him or her for a short (two to three month) mission tour? Would you? Could you? Too often, we professionals hide behind our "busy schedules" to keep from doing the good we ought to do. Let's face it—most of us probably will not be asked to go on a short mission tour in the first place, but wouldn't it be nice if we were ready to go if asked? For most of us, going to a Bible talk leaders meeting at the end of the month seems like a huge sacrifice. Sadly, many of us are not even in leadership because we do not make ourselves available.

Availability is not just a ministry issue. Are you available on the job? Do clients or patients wait interminably in your waiting room because of your poor planning? Do you return telephone calls or e-mails promptly? Are you available to pitch in and help a coworker during a crisis? I remember early on in my profession, I made a commitment not to miss any church services. There were many Wednesday nights when I would leave the fellowship and go back to the office and work for hours. One day, a partner asked if I could stay and help him prepare a witness for a trial the next day. He told me that he knew I usually was not available because of church, but that he was in a serious crunch. I offered to stay and help him with his case. (This was the only time I had ever missed church because of a job commitment.) His profound gratitude was obvious. During the ensuing years, we became close friends. When I left my law practice for a period of time, he and his wife helped to support us during the first few months of our ministry training. How about you? Are you hiding behind your profession, or are you available?

What about your financial availability? Obviously, Zenas had to be on top of his finances. Many of us would really like to get the call to do some mission work, but if we did, we would have to turn it down because we have not been prudent with our finances. In the early career years, there may be heavy education loans to repay, and we certainly need to consider our financial obligations in decisions we make. However, for many of us, we are well beyond that. Yet we are not available, not because of time or loans, but because we are living well beyond our means or beyond what is necessary.

Too many of us are not available because our things, gadgets, toys and comforts enslave us. How sad that we miss incredible opportunities to serve God and others while we fritter away the precious time God has given us, only earning money to keep up with our never ending consumption of goods. If you are not already debt free, set a goal to become so. Share it with others who are in your life. Yes, share the entire goal: every debt you owe, how long it will take to get out of each debt, and what you are willing to sacrifice. Think about how to live on less. Start saving money in order to make yourself available. Who knows when you will be called. Will you be available?

I will never forget sitting in Kip McKean's living room nearly fifteen years ago when our call came. Would I give up my law practice and become part of the ministry staff? It was the chance of a lifetime! There were many logistics to consider. I needed to talk to my law firm and clients. How would they respond? What about my family? Would we make it in the ministry? There were a thousand reasons not to jump at this opportunity; only one to go: it was God's calling. Thankfully, our financial affairs were in order. Through the generous help of friends and family, we were able to move to Boston and support ourselves for the first six months of our internship. We made ourselves available and so we answered the call. I would eventually be asked to return to the practice of law, but our lives have never been the same since.

Reliability

We need to be not only available, but also reliable. I can think of only two reasons for Paul to include Zenas with Apollos on this trip: either that Apollos was such a troublemaker that he needed a lawyer for his journey or that Paul respected Zenas as a reliable man. Many of us, as professionals, have willing hearts and make ourselves available because we truly wish to serve. Unfortunately, many of us have not learned to be reliable.

Reliability is evidenced in many ways. Do you keep your appointments? Do you finish your tasks on time? Are you on time or early to meetings? Do you end meetings when you say you are going to end? Are you thorough? Do you pay attention to details when required? Is your "yes," yes and your "no," no? (See Matthew 5:37.) There are few things more frustrating than working with a talented but unreliable man or woman. "Like a bad tooth or a lame foot is reliance on the unfaithful in times of trouble" (Proverbs 25:19).

When we commit to things and fail to follow through or do them properly, we are saying "yes" with our mouth, but "no" with our actions. We are duplicitous, which will eventually lead to destruction: "The integrity of the upright guides them, but the unfaithful are destroyed by their duplicity" (Proverbs 11:3).

I remember early in my law practice when this sin nearly caused my destruction. One of the partners had asked me to prepare a file for trial in federal court. For some reason, I did not stay on top of the file as I should have. The week before the trial, the partner called me into the office to discuss the case. I had done nearly nothing. After much well-deserved ranting and raving, he took the file from me and gave it to another associate to handle. I did not get another case from him for nearly two years, and my position in the firm for a while was tenuous at best. After that, I vowed that I would never again be unprepared for any case I had been given. I kept that vow until the day I left my practice.

Sadly, many of us would never think of dropping a ball at the office, in the courthouse or in the operating room, but we are not nearly as reliable at church. We forget our contribution and say, "I'll bring it next week." Would we say this to a judge about a brief that was due? We go weeks or months without getting together with a discipleship partner. Would you do that to a patient or client? (If so, you had better make sure that your malpractice premiums are paid up!) Would you think about missing a partnership meeting? A business opportunity? No. But, we hardly bat an eye about missing a Bible talk meeting or blowing off a Bible study.

Why this disparity? I think the bottom line is pride. Too many of us professionals are steeped in pride. We think that our agenda, our schedule and our ideas are all that really matters. Sure, we are diplomatic enough not to come right out and say it, but don't listen to your words—look at your actions. We live our lives as if our schedule is all-important and other things will simply have to wait, be skipped or rescheduled. "Don't they know that I am _____." You can fill in the blank with "busy," "traveling," "stressed," "important," "under a lot of pressure," or just plain "arrogant"! The bottom line is that the Bible says, "You are not your own; you were bought at a price. Therefore honor God with your [whatever you filled in the blank above with]." (1 Corinthians 6:19–20).

Here is a challenge: This week, treat your role in church as if it were your profession. Stop sitting around, waiting for "church" to happen. Plan your week. Set up appointments. Go into fellowship with an agenda of who you want to see and what you want to say. Use a caseload, action list, Daytimer or PDA. Take notes. Show interest in your "clients," "patients" or "customers." Follow up on them. Send them cards or letters. Call them. Take them out to a ball game. Let your "yes" be yes and your "no" be no. Who knows whose life you can change? (Maybe your own!) At the very least, you will get a kick out of all the people wondering what you are up to!

Relatability

It is amazing to me that Paul chose Zenas to accompany Apollos on this mission. It is possible that Apollos himself asked Zenas to come with him. In either case, here was a professional who had the respect and trust of spiritual men in the church leadership. Zenas must have had a close relationship with one or both of these great leaders. It saddens me that so few professionals are discipled or even known by the leaders of the church. What's up with that?

Certainly, many of our leaders choose other ministry leaders to disciple and train. But, I don't think that this is the problem. In fact, that is their job! I think something else lurks beneath these waters. Truth be told, a lot of us professionals are not discipled by ministry leaders because we are either unspiritual or we have not made ourselves valuable to the ministry. For some of us, this is intentional. We do not want the attention or the responsibility of being in a relationship like this. We prefer to hide so we can play our own agenda. For some of us, we are afraid of what we fear to be the natural outcome of having a relationship with leadership: "Pack your bags—you're off to Zimbabwe!" But unfortunately for most of us, we simply are clueless.

"Give me the case file and I'll be ready for trial by Monday." "Line up the patient and I will be in my scrubs in a heartbeat." "Show me that customer and I'll have the sales order on the desk in the morning." Most of us are professionals because we are go-getters. We know what we want and we go get it. Where is that same drive and determination when it comes to the ministry? We can go toe to toe with opposing counsel, but wilt like a two-day-old, picked daisy when it comes to talking to our evangelist or women's ministry leader. We can open a man's chest cavity, reach in and massage his heart back to life, but we do not know how to have a heart to heart talk in a discipleship time. We can close a million-dollar deal with a new client after lunch with bad breath, but we are afraid to ask our neighbor whom we have known for ten years to come to church.

Let me help you find the cure. Look into the mirror and practice saying this, "I know that I am not the spiritual man or woman I need to be. Will you let me take you out to lunch this week so you can help me be what I want to be?" Go ahead and say it. You may need to practice several times. Now, go over to the phone, call your ministry leader and say it to him or her. I'm serious! Do you want to be like Zenas? You have to pay the price. You need to humble yourself and ask for help. There is no other way.

Call your leader and talk to him or her. Ask your leader out for breakfast, lunch, dinner, whatever. Be sincere. Tell him or her you want to grow. Be honest. Get help. Become a friend. Talk to your evangelist after the sermon. Tell what you learned from his lessons. Ask questions. Think ahead. Find solutions. Volunteer. Ask a coworker or friend to church, set up a Bible study, and ask your leader to help.

Several months ago, I had a hard talk with a ministry leader who has been in my life for some time. We had grown distant and I was feeling awkward about our relationship. When I shared these things, the leader was both humble and challenging. He accepted blame for his role in our relationship. He also challenged me with these words, "The closest relationships are forged in the battle." Sadly, I understood his point. I had not been in the battle. Do you want to make yourself valuable? Pick up your spiritual weapons and get into the battle. I don't know of many ministry leaders who wouldn't die to have a Zenas in their life. You just need to be available, reliable and spiritually relatable.

Henry B. Cramer received his undergraduate degree from Stanford University and his MD from the University of California, Davis. His residency and fellowship were at the University of Illinois, Chicago, and Michigan Ear Institute, respectively. He became a Christian on April 30, 1986, in Boston, while visiting a lifelong friend, and then was brought up in the faith in the Chicago Church of Christ. He celebrated twenty years of marriage to his wife, Lanna, in June 2001, and delights in his three daughters, Lauren, Carol Anne and Dianna. He currently holds the position of chief of surgery for Pioneer Medical Group and serves as an expert reviewer for the Board of Medical Quality Assurance for the State of California.

Although an ENT doctor by professional training, Henry's devotion to service in God's kingdom moved his family to lead the church planting to Jerusalem in 1996. He currently serves as an elder and has enjoyed being a deacon and an evangelist in Los Angeles as well.

2 Luke

Partnering with the Mission

Henry B. Cramer

Exhausted, frustrated and humbled, Luke composes himself as he informs devoted parents that their three-year-old daughter is dead. Despite his best efforts, this precious child has deteriorated from excellent health to febrile illness, coma and death in less than forty-eight hours. It does not matter that he trained under Alexandria's best physicians. It is irrelevant that he did everything properly and gave up two nights of sleep attending to the needs of his tiny patient. As he shuffles home, he leaves only with the harsh and haunting truth that his best was not good enough.

He has heard bits and pieces about a Jewish teacher who not only healed the sick and lame, but even snatched back those who had succumbed to his archenemy—death. He longs to learn more about this one whom they sometimes call the Great Physician and hopes that maybe he could become the healer he always aspired to be.

Whether these were the kind of thoughts Luke had or not, he did go on to learn a great deal about Jesus and was used by God to bring a message of healing to the world. As a physician, there is much I long to learn about Luke when I meet him in heaven, but there are important characteristics about his life that can be gleaned from the Scriptures. When appreciated, these can inspire professionals to use our God-given abilities and training in order to advance the gospel of Jesus Christ. Three of Luke's most striking attributes are his devotion to excellence and accuracy, his self-initiative and his loyalty.

All-Around Excellence

Two of the most challenging aspects of medical training are the need for life-long learning and the need for accurate documentation of what we have observed or performed. All medical professionals know it is dangerous to become stagnant or complacent with one's understanding of healing while medical knowledge rapidly expands. This fact requires a persistent devotion to striving for excellence and continued development in our professional lives. It is important to note that Luke was able to transfer his devotion to excellence in medicine to outstanding achievement in his spiritual walk. His compelling and accurate account of the life, death and resurrection of Jesus Christ, along with his documentation of the activities of the first century church, serve as a lasting legacy for all those who love God (Luke 1:1–4).

Since age fifteen I had desired to be an accomplished physician. After fourteen years of education and training past high school, I was enjoying academic medicine as an attending physician at Henry Ford Hospital. I was handling challenging otologic and neurotologic cases, training otolaryngology residents, teaching medical students from the University of Michigan and Wayne State Schools of Medicine, and even occasionally flying to other cities for speaking engagements. At that point, I had been a Christian for five years, was active in my faith and had been in leadership for four and a half years. My wife, Lanna, and I and our three young daughters enjoyed being part of the church planting to Detroit (a city we San Diego natives would never have dreamed of living in prior to our conversions!). Sadly, however, my devotion to excellence in medicine far surpassed the standards I accepted for my spiritual life.

I will never forget the day when I developed a conviction about imitating Luke's excellence. I came out of the operating room one day in the summer of 1991, and a man in the waiting room handed me my first commentary—William Barclay's *The Gospel of Luke*. I was humbled that God used a stranger to get me something I should have found years prior. As I read this book during my quiet times for the next few weeks, I was amazed that this non-Jew, non-apostle, non-eyewitness wrote more words than any other author in the New Testament! Luke was extremely thorough in his historical documentation, and he recorded aspects of the life of Christ that others did not (e.g., Jesus' prayer life, treatment of the poor and his high regard for women). I reflected on my anemic efforts to be excellent in my understanding and use of the Word. I understood how little time I had spent developing greater skill and knowledge in building God's kingdom. I felt deep remorse for my shortcomings, and I asked God for forgiveness and begged for an opportunity to take it higher for him.

Within a few weeks of coming to this conviction, my wife and I accepted the invitation to move to Los Angeles in the autumn of 1991 to train for the ministry staff there. I transitioned out of academic medicine, but still worked full time as an otolaryngologist. Lanna and I devoted ourselves to learning more about serving others, as Bruce and Robyn Williams trained us to lead the Great Physician's ministry, consisting exclusively of medical professionals. Soon after our arrival in Los Angeles, we were appointed as deacon and deaconess, and later, under the training of Anthony and Saun Galang, I became the first sector leader in Los Angeles to maintain a professional career. God grew our sector, which was comprised of teens, campus, singles and marrieds, by forty percent in 1994, as we increased from 125 to 169 disciples.

By January of 1995 we were appointed evangelist and women's ministry leader. In June of 1996 we moved our family abroad to lead the church planting to Jerusalem and serve as regional directors for the faith-based charity HOPE *worldwide* in the Holy Land. What a "once in a lifetime" experience—to plant a church where Christ preached!

We were grateful to host the 1997 World Missions Leadership Conference in Jerusalem with 240 ministers from around the world in attendance, while sharing the good news with hundreds of new friends. We directed efforts for local disciples to meet the needs of the poor through service in the West Bank and Israel. I also had the privilege of doing surgery in an Orthodox Jewish Hospital while establishing a Department of Otolaryngology in the town of Beit Jala (next to Bethlehem) in a Palestinian Government Authority hospital. Later, we were asked to serve as HOPE *worldwide* vice presidents for the Middle East and eventually became geographic sector leaders for the Holy Land. We then moved back to South Central Los Angeles to train for the eldership.

Currently, Lanna and I serve as elder and women's ministry leader for more than 800 disciples in the south region of the Los Angeles Church of Christ. Our willingness to continue training for acts of service has benefited our family tremendously. Our two teenage girls (Lauren, 16, and Carol Anne, 14) are active disciples who also do well in school and sports. Our youngest daughter, twelve-year-old Dianna, thrives in an excellent preteen ministry and eagerly desires to be a disciple. I enjoy a busy practice in otolaryngology, as I head the department of surgery for a medical group of fifty physicians. However, my medical practice no longer consumes me. Lanna and I have had the privilege of sharing the good news of Jesus Christ with hundreds of people in our fifteen years as Christians and have seen more miraculous life changes than can be recorded in one book, much less one chapter. As I reflect on how God has worked in these last ten years, I am grateful for Luke's inspiring example and his quest for excellence that deepened my convictions.

Stellar Self-Initiative

Through much of our education in medicine, physicians usually do what those training us tell us to do. It is impressive that Luke exhibited great self-initiative by taking it upon himself to chronicle the activities of Jesus and the first century church.

> Therefore, since I myself have carefully investigated everything from the beginning, it seemed good also to me to write an orderly account for you, most excellent Theophilus, so that you may know the certainty of the things you have been taught. (Luke 1:3–4)

It was not as if Luke had trained for this incredibly important task. As a Gentile, he did not have access to a rich heritage of documenting the works of God. Luke was not an apostle or even an eyewitness to the incidents of his Gospel. What compelled him to undertake such an enormous project? Of course, the Holy Spirit must have put this on Luke's heart. However, there have been many things impressed upon my heart that I have never pursued. Somewhere in his life Luke developed the *deep conviction* that God was preparing him for works of service that no one else was going to do. He must have believed that there was not going to be a Gospel account written by a Gentile unless he did it. There was not going to be a well-organized history of the first century church unless he did it. Luke took responsibility for figuring out what God wanted him to do and got busy doing it. We know that Luke traveled with Paul on parts of his journeys (Acts 16:10 and 20:6, note the use of "we") and made the final journey to Rome with him (Acts 27:1) and that he probably did not need to wait for Paul to write later to the church at Ephesus to understand the following:

> For it is by grace you have been saved, through faith—and this not from yourselves, it is the gift of God—not by works, so that no one can boast. For we are God's workmanship, created in Christ Jesus to do good works, which God prepared in advance for us to do. (Ephesians 2:8–10)

Back in 1997, I was fortunate to have dinner with Wyndham Shaw, one of the congregational elders for the Boston Church of Christ. During the meal, I was discussing my dilemma of how best to serve the kingdom. Wyndham explained it for me by suggesting that I needed to figure out what I was uniquely qualified to do. Too often in my spiritual life I have only done what I have been asked to do. This is helpful in building up the body of Christ—to a certain degree. However, on another level, God needs his servants to wrestle with the specific tasks that he has prepared for them.

The most recent example of this is my involvement with the HOPE *worldwide* Health Corps. In 1987, God put it on my heart (through meeting with Roger Lamb) that there should be a medical ministry within the International Churches of Christ. In various capacities, I have helped support the development of such an entity. I have led medical ministries in Los Angeles and served in health-related programs in and outside of the United States. I helped organize the precursor to the HOPE *worldwide* Health Corps held in Los Angeles in 1995 and have attended every Health Corps, including the most recent meeting held in February of 2001 in Phnom Penh, Cambodia. Each conference has been better and better and more and more inspiring.

All five members of my immediate family as well as my mom, dad and sister (a retired general surgeon) attended this most recent conference in Cambodia, directed by Graham and Suzanne Gumley. The excellence of the scientific presentations was evidenced by certification for fifteen Continuing Medical Education (CME) credits through the University of Southern California School of Medicine. As fantastic as this life-changing experience was for those in attendance, I was saddened that there were only 176 participants. I saw how tired many of the medical professionals looked who had been serving in HOPE *worldwide* programs around the world. They were still very zealous for the work, but it was obvious that they were carrying too much of the load without reinforcements.

Here is where I needed to follow Luke's example. With the help of many others, I was able to plan a spiritual conference for medical professionals that will be held about the time this book is released. It was very clear to me that I was uniquely qualified to build consensus in the body of Christ for a different type of HOPE *worldwide* Health Corps for 2002, and it was equally clear that I needed to take the initiative. Most of you reading this book have been well-prepared by God to make a crucial difference in some area. Be an imitator of Luke and take the initiative. Step out and let God use you.

Lifelong Loyalty

Finally, I am struck by Luke's loyalty to God and Paul. If we are going to partner with the mission as medical professionals, then we had better learn the importance of remaining faithful through challenging experiences. My guess is that, at times, Paul could be a difficult person to get along with out on the mission field. However, we know from Colossians 4:14 that Luke hung in there with Paul until the end. Others deserted Paul, but not Luke.

What is it about medical professionals that prepares them to work with highly ambitious people with forceful personalities? Perhaps it has something to do with our training. To this day, I am indebted for all that my teachers in medicine imparted to me. They were not perfect people. Several died from AIDS acquired through their lifestyle choices. Some had substance abuse problems. Many were prideful, arrogant and had wicked tempers. However, they all knew more than I did about healing and were kind enough to teach me. For this, I am eternally grateful.

Here comes the convicting part. I eventually developed shame that I was so willing to put up with the challenging personalities of those who trained me in medicine but I was so quick to cop an attitude with God's leaders when they tried to train me to be more godly. What is even more embarrassing is that despite my best efforts, I can be a tremendous pain to be around, myself! Many of the attributes that make for a great surgeon (brutal honesty, attention to minute detail and insistence on excellence) can make for a lousy husband, father, leader and friend. Hardly a day goes by when I do not see my shortcomings more clearly. I am thankful that one of the heroes of Luke's Gospel is a tax collector who was justified because he was willing to say, "God be merciful to me, a sinner" (Luke 18:13–14). Fortunately, like Luke, I have also learned from Paul:

> We who are strong ought to bear with the failings of the weak and not to please ourselves. Each of us should please his neighbor for his good, to build him up. For even Christ did not please himself but, as it is written: "The insults of those who insult you have fallen on me." For everything that was written in the past was written to teach us, so that through endurance and the encouragement of the Scriptures we might have hope.
>
> May the God who gives endurance and encouragement give you a spirit of unity among yourselves as you follow Christ Jesus,

so that with one heart and mouth you may glorify the God and Father of our Lord Jesus Christ.

Accept one another, then, just as Christ accepted you, in order to bring praise to God. (Romans 15:1–7)

Somewhere along the line, I am confident Luke figured out that the only way he was going to partner with the mission was to understand and work on his own shortcomings, while bearing with those of others. I have been forgiven of so much sin before and after my conversion that it would be a horrible insult to Christ to not remain loyal to the calling he set before me. I am grateful for the example of Luke and the exciting challenge of partnering with the ministry, as together we work to bring about healing in the ways of the Great Physician.

Luke prepared himself to bring healing to men's bodies, but he did not allow knowledge to puff him up. He stayed humble before God and before others whom God put in this life. And God enabled him to stay in the race and did more through him than he could ask or imagine. The impact of his work is still felt today around the world. In his Gospel and his life he held up a powerful principle of Jesus. It is certainly for all people, but one especially important to us well-trained professionals:

"For everyone who exalts himself will be humbled, and he who humbles himself will be exalted." (Luke 14:1)

Kitty Chiles received her bachelor of arts degree from Skidmore College. She became a disciple in 1990 in Tallahasse, Florida. She is a vice president of HOPE *worldwide*, overseeing the programs in the ACES (Africa, Caribbean, Empire States and Southeast US) World Sector, parallel to the churches in the International Churches of Christ, along with her husband, Bud.

Prior to working for HOPE *worldwide*, Kitty was co-owner and vice president of Chiles Communications, Inc., a governmental relations firm in Florida. In addition to running political campaigns, the firm was involved in many of Florida's critical state issues such as the fight for interstate banking, the effort to block the construction of an environmentally dangerous natural gas pipeline across Florida's aquifer, and the protection of endangered species such as the manatee. She was a member of the Florida council to raise funds to restore Ellis Island, and served as a board member of Florida House, the state's Washington Embassy. Additionally, Kitty acted as a codeveloper of The Governor's Inn, an exclusive hotel in Tallahassee, Florida, and numerous office buildings in the state capital. She and Bud have been married for more than twenty-five years and have three children, Lawton, Katie and Geoffrey.

3 Tabitha

The Joy of Giving

Kitty Chiles

As the dawn light pierced her room, Tabitha rose from her mat. It had been a late night. In spite of her own weariness, she was so glad that she had waited up for the men to return from hearing Peter preach in Lydda. She had used the time well, finishing the last stitches on the widow Anna's robe in time for tonight's wedding festivities. Since the death of her husband, it had been so difficult for Anna to put food on the table, let alone buy a suitable robe for her daughter's wedding. Tabitha hoped that Anna would be pleased with what she had made. All the years she had spent learning the intricate stitches of her trade had made Tabitha the most sought after seamstress in all of Joppa.

She had taken special care to incorporate her finest work into Anna's robe. Many times she had made clothes for Anna's children, but this indeed would be something special. It gave her great pleasure to give Anna a gift that she would never be able to buy on her own. The robe would signify the beginning of a new life for Anna, as she would finally have a family to care for her again.

Just as she was finishing the last stitches, the men had returned from Lydda. How thrilling to see the excitement on their faces as they spoke of their visit to the temple, relaying every word of Peter's message. What a privilege for her husband to hear the words of a man who had walked with our Lord! Surely, she was blessed among women to once again hear of Jesus' appearing to the disciples after his death. She could not wait to find the time to tell all the other women all she had heard; they would be so encouraged.

Hearing the good news always took her back to the moment when the blue waters of the Mediterranean Sea washed over her in baptism, as she took on the life of following the ways of Jesus. Cut to the heart by Jesus' humble nature, Tabitha had decided to die to the old way of putting herself first. How many times she had renewed her pledge to God since that day! Her life had been so full since then! There were so many needs around her, especially those of the widows whom she had come to know and love so dearly. And, even though it was challenging to fit their needs in to her days with her family and the demands of her profession, she knew that God had chosen her to see and meet these needs, and she felt a great joy to be a part of their lives.

Enough contemplation for now! If she did not hurry, the children would be late for their lessons. She only had until next week to finish the gown for the mayor's wife.

❖

The first reference to Tabitha in the book of Acts tells me quite a lot about her: she was a "disciple" and was "always doing good and helping the poor" (Acts 9:36). A little research reveals that Tabitha is the only woman in the New Testament specifically described as a disciple. While this does not mean that she was the *only* female disciple, it occurred to me that God may have intended to confer a special honor on Tabitha through this, and it made me want to understand her even more.

Pure, Faultless Religion

Tabitha must have had eyes that saw and ears that heard the needs of others. She must have been a woman whom people were drawn to, someone to whom they entrusted their friendship and their emptiness. However, perceiving needs is only the first step to meeting them. "Always doing good" is no simple task. It requires forethought and planning, creativity and hard work, mustering resources and time—aspects of our lives that we are tempted to reserve for ourselves. We are often challenged by extending ourselves for our families and for the lost, leaving the energy, time and resources we give to the poor and needy for special and infrequent days. Tabitha, with her heart for the needy, has an important lesson for all of us.

Tabitha must have been a woman who denied herself every day in order to weave the needs of these women into her life. Her service was not so much something she did; it must have become who she was. The widows had only their gratitude and friendship to give back to her, and I am sure there were times when neither was forthcoming. I believe Tabitha's needs were being met by God, which allowed her to serve those with very little to give back. She was a devoted follower of Jesus, a disciple who modeled herself after our Lord, and a woman who made helping others her way of life.

Central among those Tabitha helped were the widows who mourned her death and spoke about her to Peter when he arrived in Joppa at their beckoning. In various places in the New Testament, we hear mention of the widows who were part of the fellowship in the various churches and are told of their needs. They were traditionally outcasts of society, left to fend for themselves if they were without extended family. The Scriptures describe the care of "widows in their distress" as "religion that God our Father accepts as pure and faultless" (James 1:27). Tabitha was a woman who took those commands to heart and made caring for these women part of her life.

Following her death, along with their tears, they displayed the clothing she had made for them to Peter. They would miss her deeply. In the midst of all of her other responsibilities, her family, her career, her ministry, Tabitha had found the heart and the time to seek and meet the needs of these women. Their grief is a testament to the relationship of care and concern that she had built with them. Ordinarily they could have accepted the death of a friend. However, Tabitha was no ordinary friend. She had so woven herself into the hearts and lives of these needy women that they were compelled to go to Peter in hopes of a miracle.

Tabitha entrusted her life to God, but what gave her life such power was her re-affirmation of this pledge every day. Serving was not just a task or a ritual. She went beyond the expectations of the people around her and gave her heart to the needy. She sought after people who had little to give back.

Seeing My Need

Before I became a Christian, most of my relationships were based on what I could get, not on what I could give. At that time in my life, I was in the sixth year of my marriage, running a business with my husband, and living the life with few cares. We had it all—the nice home, the nice cars, even the nice airplane. Though we made the "politically correct" donations every so often, we were ignorant of the giving heart that God desires.

My first encounter with Jesus came in the form of Carla Armstrong, a disciple in Tallahassee, Florida. Even though she was a temporary secretary and I was her "boss," she did not hesitate to reach out to me and build a friendship. For more than a year, we met for lunch once a week to study the Bible, and she gently taught God's word to my completely unschooled mind and heart. I remember being amazed that she would give her time and knowledge to me, expecting nothing in return. God was giving me my first lesson in sacrificial giving.

Despite these times in God's word, I remained blind to my need for God. In October 1981, I went into labor five and one half months early in my first pregnancy. After being flown by helicopter to a nearby hospital, my husband and I were told that nothing could be done to stop the labor from commencing. The baby would have a two percent chance of survival. Suddenly, my need for God had become very apparent! Lawton was born at one pound, two ounces. Each day of his life, he hung on by a tiny thread. Each day I realized more and more how little the doctors could do, how dependent my child's life was on God's mercy, and how completely undeserving I was of that mercy. I was beginning to understand that I had no real control over the way my life was going and that only God could meet my needs.

Even though Lawton was in the hospital many more months, knowing he was so clearly in God's hands helped me to focus on doing what I needed to do—become his daughter through baptism. God had known exactly what I needed in order to see my need for him. Like Tabitha, I had realized that God is the ultimate provider. Four months after his birth (and mine!) we were able to bring Lawton home. God had not only met Lawton's physical needs, but my spiritual needs as well. Little did I know how much God would continue to mold me to become more like him in meeting the needs of others.

Meeting Others' Needs

As a disciple in Tallahassee, I participated in once a year outreaches to the poor and gave to special collections when the opportunities arose. Not until we were asked to move to New York and work for HOPE *worldwide* did I see how far I was from having the heart of Tabitha. She willingly gave everything: time, money and energy. Yet I struggled with the same sacrifices that she took such joy in. Doing my job was not the problem; working the needs of the poor and the resulting relationships into the fabric of my everyday life was the challenge. Tabitha gave out of a daily gratitude for God. Every single morning Tabitha must have woken up and set her heart on being grateful that all her needs were already met. This is the only way she could have lived each day "*always* doing good" (Acts 9:36, emphasis added). This daily renewal of her heart is the quality in her that is most convicting to me.

Even now, ten years after beginning our work for the poor, I find the daily commitment challenging. All the training, education, experience and knowledge in the world cannot make me a woman like Tabitha. While each of us has a list of things we need to accomplish each workday, only *God's Spirit* and faith in his provision leads me to deny myself and help someone when it is not part of my to-do list. Helping the family of a dying child settle into an apartment was gratifying, but fitting a monthly visit into my crazy life proves to be very challenging. I knew that these were the true tests for my heart: helping the poor in ways that required me to set myself aside on a daily basis. At these times, I am even more in awe of Tabitha's commitment to the poor.

As I look back over the last ten years, the times when I went beyond meeting the needs of my family, my job and my neighbors to help someone are some of the times I am the most proud of. They were times when I remember feeling as if I was fulfilling the call to discipleship in a more complete way. As a disciple living in the United States, I have been susceptible to Satan's accusations that I live the comfortable life. When I am involved with the poor in a personal way, Satan loses this foothold in my life; my giving of myself sets me free.

People, Not Tasks

I have found that the relationships I build with others are a thread of substance, winding itself through all the tasks of my day and giving it meaning. My friendships with the poor are especially meaningful, as my eyes have been opened to all the false barriers Satan erects between us. God intends for me to interrupt my busy-ness and "always" do good by giving to others what they need. In so doing, my needs have been met as well. As professionals, I think, at times it is easy to be task-oriented and focused on what we can accomplish. Even in helping the poor, my "self" and what "I" can do so easily creep into my day. God intends that each of us works to push ourselves—and Satan's reasoning—out of the way.

It must have been tempting for Tabitha to shut out the needs of those around her. We too can easily become weary of doing good. We can see serving as a burden, a hardship, and fail to grasp the incredible rewards of giving from a selfless heart. When Tabitha looked at Jesus, she saw someone who poured himself out every day, even to the point of death. Her determination to mirror the example of her Lord has brought her the honor of being one of the extraordinary women of the New Testament. Tabitha glorified God by using every talent and resource that God had given her to display the character of Jesus. By giving our time and heart to the poor, we too can demonstrate the power of Jesus' love, glorifying him with our lives and bringing great joy to others and ourselves.

David Banks graduated from the University of Indiana with a bachelor's degree in chemistry and from the University of California, San Diego, with a master's in chemistry. He received his MBA from Purdue University. He has thirty-two years of corporate experience, seventeen of which were in general management of high technology companies. He has extensive international business experience in Europe, Taiwan, China and Japan, balancing small and large company experience, with thirteen years at large firms and nineteen years at startups, on both coasts. He was the founding general partner of a venture fund focused on optical technologies. David has been a board director or chairman of fourteen organizations, two of which were nonprofits—including HOPE *worldwide* San Francisco.

Married thirty-two years to his wife, Jan, they have two grown children, Christina and Douglas. Christina is married to Gary Simmons and they lead the Fresno Church of Christ. David became a disciple in 1995 in San Francisco.

4 Barnabas

Just One Disciple

David Banks

Throughout the Bible, we see examples of how God can work powerfully through one person. Barnabas is just such an example. He plays a vital role in Paul's ministry in the first century church. Who is this Joseph, called Barnabas or "Son of Encouragement"? The Scriptures give us a list of attributes that answer this question.

The Bible's very first mention of Barnabas demonstrates his *sacrificial* heart (Acts 4:36–37). He sold his field and gave the money to the apostles. Then, in Acts 9:26–27, we see how *courageous* Barnabas was because he persuaded the apostles to accept the radical new convert, Paul. Acts 11:23 describes how *encouraging* Barnabas was to the leaderless Antioch church prior to Paul's arrival. Full of faith and the Holy Spirit, he epitomized what it is to be *spiritual* (Acts 11:24). A visionary, Barnabas was the catalyst for Paul's first missionary journey when he brought Paul to the Antioch church, *inspiring* both Paul and that church (Acts 11:25–26). In Acts 11:29–30 the church in Antioch sends its contribution to Jerusalem with Barnabas, having found him *trustworthy*. The Holy Spirit teams up Paul and Barnabas to evangelize both Jews and Gentiles, an indication that Barnabas shares Paul's *evangelistic* heart (Acts 13:2). Along with Paul, Barnabas was *self-supporting*, as described in 1 Corinthians 9:6, not relying on financial support from the church.

Barnabas uses these qualities to become many things to Paul. Barnabas was a *guide* to Paul in at least two ways. He vouched for Paul before Peter and the apostles, and he led Paul to his first church at Antioch. No doubt, Paul used Barnabas as his *advisor*—perhaps on matters of appointing leaders in nascent churches.

43

The man "out front" always needs an *encourager* and Barnabas proved true to his name throughout Acts 13–15. Barnabas became an *example* for Paul. After Paul refuses to take John Mark with them, Barnabas discipled John Mark to the extent that Paul ended up recommending him to the Colossian church (Colossians 4:10).

❖❖❖

The older of two boys, I was fortunate enough to grow up in a close family. My dad was a depression-era son of a farmer who chose a thirty-five-year career with the Social Security Administration because it seemed "safe." My mother was a life-time Christian Scientist, a teacher and a devoted wife. We all went to the Christian Science church because Dad had no spiritual convictions. For most of my childhood we lived the kind of life captured in 1950s TV shows like *Father Knows Best* and *Ozzie and Harriet*.

The event that pretty much defined the next forty years of my life occurred the summer I turned twelve. While on summer vacation, my typical summer bronchitis bout turned ugly, and I had a serious asthma attack that required my hospitalization. Since Mom was a Christian Scientist, this proved to be a major crisis for her faith. Medical treatment by doctors won out over Christian Science doctrine, birthing my skepticism regarding "organized" religion.

Fighting Back

That summer was just the beginning. My sometimes loud breathing became the source of jokes amongst some of my classmates. For much of the eighth grade I was not able to participate in sports, dances or even hang-out times. I became bitter, vengeful and very hard-hearted. During this time, Dad fought to get me into the most advanced research program in the nation, the Jewish National Home for Asthmatic Children. Formerly a US relocation center for children of the Holocaust, the JNHAC was a residential, two-year program in Denver that sought to return asthmatic children to a life as normal and active as possible. The home was my first experience at group living and forced me to build and maintain strong relationships. As my health improved, I could engage in sports for the first time, which greatly improved my confidence.

After returning from the home to my home in Indiana, I drove myself to excel, eager to compensate for what I'd lost because of illness. I attended Indiana University, the University of California at San Diego and Purdue, acquiring an education, good friends, job offers and, along the way, an amazing wife named Janice. I was out of school and working my first job at Hewlett Packard (HP) in September of 1969.

Success at Any Cost

I put work ahead of Jan for the next twenty-six years. This me-first approach to life made Jan's life very lonely because I was unwilling to emotionally engage her. Jan was pregnant with our first child, Christina, while I was mapping out career moves that I was sure would result in my becoming CEO of HP. We moved eight times, to wherever the company sent me. Our son, Doug, was born when Chris was twenty-one months old. In my twelfth year at HP, my mentor left the company and my fast-track advancements came to a screeching halt—just when Jan decided to seek a divorce. However, she relented and we remained a family for the next thirteen years, during which I was the CEO of three technology startup companies. Versant, the third startup, was eight months from going public in July of 1995 when I turned fifty. From the outside, I had more of everything than I had ever dreamed of. On the inside I felt empty, sad and without direction. I had not yet become a Barnabas, but was a work in process.

Redefining Success

Jan met some disciples, studied the Bible and was baptized while we lived in Rhode Island in 1988, during my second startup. At age forty-one, she became the spiritual leader of our family. Jan became less critical, more forgiving and had greater joy than any time in our marriage. Doug was baptized at age fif-teen, one month after Jan, and Chris was baptized at age nine-teen while at Colorado University in Boulder. While I respected the children's decision, it felt like my family wanted me to make a decision that I was not ready to make.

God used two powerful disciples to change my heart: Russ Ewell and Tonnis Wildeboer. The Ewells had moved to the Bay Area in 1993, where we had lived since 1992, to lead the San Francisco church. I found it very difficult to ignore Russ' power-ful preaching. Between his challenging messages and Tonnis Wildeboer's prayers, I had no alternative but to study the Bible. Tonnis asked me to study—and nine days later, on August 19, 1995, I was baptized by my son. Jan had been faithful for seven years until God answered her prayers for her "holdout husband" to find God. Russ and I had lunch and got to know one another two weeks after my baptism. That is when I found my "Paul."

A 'Barnabas' in Process

Manufacturing has a term that describes incomplete assem-blies as "work in process." This term describes my education and professional life. At fifty-six years of age, I can now look back and see God's hand in preparing me to help the kingdom as a busi-ness professional.

The objective of my graduate education was to obtain a PhD in organic chemistry, which I was one year away from complet-ing. Being in love with someone 2500 miles away, however, caused a late course correction. A PhD became a master's in chemistry. I then returned to Indiana, near Jan, for an MBA pro-gram at Purdue. I have since concluded that (1) God wanted me to marry this woman who would eventually lead me to him; and (2) God wanted me to be a businessman, not a scientist.

Hewlett Packard extensively interviewed on campus and after my interview, I desperately wanted to go work for the company at its Palo Alto, California, headquarters. The problem was they wanted electrical and mechanical engineers, and I was a chemist. A San Francisco plant visit to Crown Zellerbach opened the door for me to finagle an HP interview that led to my first, full-time job offer. HP was at a $300 million per year revenue-run rate, but felt like a small company. It had a unique culture embodied in a statement called the HP Way which put priority on profit, employee dignity and community service. I was sure I could grow into an executive officer and then the top job. Thanks to a mentor, it looked like my plan was on track, until the mentor left HP to start his own company. It took about eighteen months for me to realize that I was not going to be a division manager, let alone HP's future CEO. The thirteen years in which I had given HP top priority in my life had nearly broken up our family. While it felt a lot like failure at the time, I now see how God protected our family and had other plans for my career.

The call that pulled me out of HP was from an executive search firm. A very small machine vision company in New Jersey was looking for a marketing vice president. I took the call, interviewed and accepted the position. My family moved to Princeton, New Jersey, where we spent three years while I learned the hard way that Object Recognition Systems (ORS) was definitely not HP. ORS was more of a financial promotion than it was a real company. When the board of directors uncovered this truth, it asked me to manage the company until it could find a legal way out of trouble. As soon as we found an experienced CEO, I alerted my network that I was looking. Since ORS had gone public in the heady times of the early '80s, many shareholders sued the company. Inexplicably, however, I was the only executive not named as a defendant. Again, God protected our family from the consequences of my bad decision in joining this company.

Executives in startup businesses are a lot like NFL coaches. When you do not succeed at one place, another place recruits you and you have a new chance to start again. Our next stop was Providence, Rhode Island, where Cadre Technologies recruited me to be their CEO. My children, Chris and Doug, were in high school, and I had promised them no moves until they completed their senior years. (Actually, I made that promise in Princeton and broke it when we moved to Providence.) Our family loved

Providence and Cadre. I took the company from eight people and no revenue to 120 people and $15 million in revenue.

Meanwhile, Jan was working as a neonatal ICU nurse at the local hospital. She started attending the Providence Church of Christ and soon thereafter began studying the Bible. The children excelled. Chris graduated and went off to UC Boulder. Doug was baptized, was valedictorian of his class and was accepted at the University of Pennsylvania.

I then made another bonehead move and merged Cadre with a firm in Oregon and found myself forced out of the company a few years later by the man I had approved as CEO of the combined company. Cadre validated the most important lesson I had learned at HP directly from Bill Hewlett, "People are the most important ingredient in business, as they are in life." God was beginning to get my attention.

By now, you probably get the pattern. We moved from Providence back to Silicon Valley, less than twenty miles from where Jan and I started our married life. I became CEO of Versant. The growth of the Internet required an expanded telecommunications infrastructure. These trends played to Versant's technology, so I pointed the company at the world's top five telecommunication companies. Versant's revenues grew rapidly enough to get us profitable and to enable our selling shares to go public in July of 1996. Like Barnabas, I was very capable in the buying and selling arena, but I had not yet learned to use that ability for God. Still unknown to me, I was a work in process.

Power Lunch

Let's go back to 1995 and my first lunch with Russ Ewell. What difference can just one day make? Well, that day we discussed company growth dynamics, the role professionals could play in the kingdom, the emergence of the Internet and my firm convictions regarding a significant kingdom Web presence. My guiding Russ in this direction ultimately led to the creation of www.icoc.org, dozens of individual church Web sites throughout the world, and ultimately, the NET World Sector[1] of the

International Churches of Christ. As God used Barnabas with Paul, God was using me as a catalyst to kick off another mission!

Then in 1996, Russ took me to an administrators' conference in Los Angeles where I met Cecil Wooten, John Bringardner, Al Baird and Kip McKean. Of course, his purpose in asking me was not just the conference. It was to share ideas and gain encouragement about the organizational improvements he had planned for the San Francisco church. However, Russ's thinking was, as usual, way beyond mine.

During my six years as a disciple, I have been considered trustworthy enough to chair the board of directors for HOPE *worldwide* San Francisco as well as hold a seat on the NET World Sector's board of directors.

In early 2000, Jan and I joined about forty couples at the church office where Russ presented his vision for the NET World Sector. During the rest of 2000, the "New Media" in NET became UpCyberDown, the online community of the International Churches of Christ; the "Exceptional Children" portion became the Hope Technology Group School; and the "Technology" branch became Genesis, the production engine that manages content for UpCyberDown. But Russ pointed out just one small problem as the NET got underway: there was no budget for this new world sector's first partial year of existence.

Having co-led an executive fellowship group in the church, I had a good idea of who the financially blessed families were. With church leadership approval, I asked about fifteen couples to meet at the church office where we agreed to donate a combined total of more than $700,000 to *fund* the birth of the NET World Sector.

Eternal Impact

Most new disciples who are professionals believe their impact will primarily be with the skills and experience God has provided throughout their careers. But God's vision is much greater. Just as the Bible speaks of Barnabas and Paul early in Acts, I came into the kingdom with guidance to give Russ about the Web, scaling organizations and business. Later, the Bible speaks of Paul and

Barnabas, with Paul leading the way. Russ and his wife, Gail, have been instrumental in spiritually leading Jan and me through some very rough waters during the past two years. We learned that we also need to be examples in *evangelism*. After a slow start, Jan and I have been fruitful with four couples who have in turn provided spiritual grandchildren. Indeed, every disciple who was involved in the launch of the NET has helped others to become disciples. To God be the glory!

Lessons I Have Learned

- 1 Corinthians 12:12–31 is true. God works through every member of Christ's body, including men and women in business, medicine, law, education and other professions.
- God calls us according to his time, not ours, and to his purpose. Had I become CEO of HP, I believe that I would have lost my family, never would have become a disciple and would have lived an empty life.
- Failure is not fatal! On the contrary, career failures can often be seen through life's rearview mirror as God's unfolding plan for our lives. Every step in my career has contributed to my ability to help the kingdom and personally make disciples.
- Disciples who are professionals today can make a great difference in God's kingdom, just as Barnabas did in Paul's ministry in the first century church.

Who is Barnabas? Just one person, a "work in process," helping to advance the kingdom. I thank God for the high calling.

Note

[1]NET stands for "New Media," "Exceptional Children" and "Technology."

District court judge Kris D. Bailey is married to his wife of twenty years, Terri. They have been blessed with two children, Mariah, 14, and Jordan, 12. Kris grew up in a God-fearing home in the Southeast US. He graduated from Freed-Hardeman University in 1978 and went on to do graduate work at Clemson University where he was baptized into Christ in 1979. In 1995 he received his JD in law from the University of Georgia. In November 2000, Kris was elected (in a recount by less than one percent!) to the District Court of North Carolina.

Kris is a deacon in the Triangle church in Raleigh, North Carolina, a Special Olympics volunteer, a HOPE for Kids volunteer and a youth soccer coach. He is particularly honored to serve in the same court with the Honorable Bill Lawton, who will be contributing to volume 2 of this work.

5 Pilate

For Want of Integrity

Kris D. Bailey

W e don't name our children or pets "Pilate." Nobody has an "Uncle Pilate." When we think of Pilate, the words "spineless," "typical politician" and "coward" come to mind. We don't think of strength, integrity or courage.

Pontius Pilate was the Rome-appointed governor over Judea (Palestine) from 26–36 AD, an unusually long period for governors. He was not only the Roman administrator of the region, but he also exercised supreme judicial power. His rule ended only when Caesar recalled him to Rome in 36 AD because of unrest in Samaria.

A significant part of Pilate's role as Roman governor was that of judge. Palestine, being under Roman occupation, had a Supreme Court of one: Pilate. There was no jury. Pilate was judge and jury. Today we call that "summary judgment"—swift, certain, final. His decisions were rarely appealed and needed no committee for approval. As a district court judge, I can relate to Pilate. I am the judge and jury most of the time because most of the trials at the district court level are "bench trials." There is no jury, and the judge decides the law and facts.

Being a judge is an interesting experience, especially for a Christian. From some angles it would seem that I have the best job in the world. Think about it. I'm never late for work because court can't start without me. Court can only start when the judge gets there. (As an attorney, I would often say in open court, if the judge was not there when court was scheduled to start, "Your Honor, you are not late, we are just early!" That would always bring a grin of agreement from the judge.)

A judge never worries much about what to wear. "Let's see, shall I wear the black robe today, or shall I wear the other black robe?" When I walk into the room, an armed deputy raises his voice and, strangely, everyone stands up. They call me, "Your Honor" scores of times every day in court...and at the local grocery store, Wal-Mart, restaurants, football games, at church and at neighborhood cookouts.

Since my election as district court judge in North Carolina, I have never told a joke that was not hilarious—everybody laughs at the judge's jokes. Grown men with gray hair who make a lot more money than I do, stand when they address me. If I raise my hand palm side facing them, they stop immediately in midsentence, on a dime. When I lower my hand, they start talking again. A judge gets the final word, always. Not only the final word, but also, even the losing attorney often says, "Thank you, Your Honor." A judge gets the final word and very rarely will anyone confront him about his decision. In some ways it is scary that anyone is given such authority and such control.

At times we all can relate to Pilate. He was out there on an island; he had to decide on his own. You and I as parents, as well as in various roles in the workplace, like Pilate, have to make the call. Sometimes we decide what will happen to whom and when.

Pilate sat in the "judge's seat." (Matthew 27:19) In my courtroom, the "judge's seat" is on a platform with a huge desk and is the biggest and best chair with the best view in the room. Nobody sits in the judge's seat but the judge. Moreover, the judge does not just have an office; he has "chambers." If I shut the door to my chambers, nobody dares come in, and only a brave few dare to even knock; and if they knock, they do so very softly, respectfully. If the judge is taking a nap, that soft, respectful knock will rarely wake him. (I know.)

In addition to all this pomp and circumstance, a judge has raw power. I have a deputy with a gun loaded with bullets (do not think Barney Fife, etc.) whose job is to guard and protect me. Don't think for a minute that this doesn't get to your head every now and then!

Pilate had the power and the control that many people want. However, Pilate lacked an essential ingredient that the role of judge, as well as every other role our lives demands: integrity.

Integrity 101

Integrity can be defined as "unimpaired moral principles, honesty and soundness, the quality of being whole or undivided." Pilate, while in authority, surely lacked integrity. His moral principles were impaired. He was not honest (not even with himself), he was unsound and he was divided.

As a judge, I have the best job in the world, but I also have the worst job in the world! I must make the decision. I have no committee to blame it on, no cover. It can be the worst job because you can never slip in the back way, a little late, after the meeting has started. Everybody knows when you are late! It can be the worst job because of the dress, a black robe: bland, unflattering, no color or style. A judge spends years telling jokes that aren't really funny, but everybody "laughs" anyway.

A judge rarely gets corrected, even when he is clearly wrong. Once in open court before a packed courtroom, I rescheduled a case and confidently set the date as February 31. Nobody said anything, but it did get very quiet. Once every four years you can schedule a case for February 29, but February 31 just will never work!

More seriously, the authority of the "judge's seat," "chambers," and the "inherent power of contempt" easily lends itself to pride in the judge's heart. And pride comes just before the fall. The deputy with the gun and bullets? He does not follow me to the grocery store, Wal-Mart, restaurants, football games, church and neighborhood cookouts. So, Pilate and I can relate to having the best/worst job in the world. A job that demands, tests and ultimately stands on the character trait of integrity.

Integrity is put to its purest test when you or I, like Pilate, have to make decisions alone, decisions that fall within our power and discretion. As Jesus stood in judgment before Pilate, Pilate's true lack of integrity was revealed as he dealt with the approval or disapproval of others, the inevitable cost of his decision about Jesus and truth.

Ignoring the Crowds

Pilate was concerned with the opinion of the crowd (Mark 15:5). Integrity is concerned with doing what is right, no matter the reaction of any group or individual. The approval or disapproval of others does not validate or invalidate integrity. Pilate knew what was right (Matthew 27:18–19) and was willing to do right, only as long as it did not start an uproar or decrease his popularity with the Jewish leaders or with Caesar.

As a candidate for judge (my position is an elected one in my state), this principle was put to an unsuspected test. Shortly after my decision to enter the election process, an attorney friend of mine saw me at the courthouse and asked where to "send the check." As a novice candidate, I asked what he meant. You see, in North Carolina our Code of Judicial Conduct and our campaign laws allow for attorneys to make campaign contributions to judges' election campaigns. That's the law. That's business as usual. Some might call it the "good ole boy network." I did not like the idea of hearing a case in which an attorney before me had given my campaign a thousand dollars. The problem is obvious and undeniable. Therefore, I decided to refuse any contributions from lawyers. Please do not think me noble because this decision was yet to be tested. At the time I made that decision, I did not fully understand its implications.

First, my opponent, a fourteen-year incumbent would raise close to $50,000, mostly from lawyers; my campaign, zero from lawyers—a disadvantage to say the least! However, the test of fire would come when the local print, TV and radio media ran stories favorable to my position. What was the "crowd's" reaction? The president of the local bar wrote a letter to the editor critical of me; lawyers who have habitually given to judge's campaigns refused to talk to me and vowed to "get me." Most disturbingly, several sitting judges whom I respect and who had quietly taken campaign money from lawyers gave me the cold shoulder. One judge even filed a complaint with the State Judicial Standards Commission, subjecting me to possible disciplinary action.

Did it hurt? Yes. Did I like the disdain of my fellow attorneys and the disapproval of my fellow judges? No. It hurt. In a way, I backed myself into a "good" corner by taking the "no money from lawyers stand" early, long before I could understand the full implications of that decision. It was stressful to stand alone. I can relate to Pilate. Nevertheless, integrity does not concern itself with the approval or disapproval of others. (By the way, with the Lord's obvious help, we won by less than one percent—in a recount!)

Having No Price

Integrity does not care about the price. Neither the amount of money nor the risk to prestige or position sways integrity. Pilate knew what was right and even wanted—and tried—to set Jesus free (John 19:12). However, Pilate would do so only if the price to himself was minimal. When the crowd said, "If you let this man go, you are no friend of Caesar," then the price for Pilate was set. Doing right and releasing Jesus would result in unrest and an unfavorable report to Rome. Sadly, this became an easy decision for a typical politician.

Children see integrity (or sadly, the lack of integrity) as they watch their parents lives. They see detail and principles— whether good or bad—and their character is thereby profoundly influenced. Do they see integrity in you? My dad, Tom Bailey, passed on in 1996. He taught me something about integrity. I watched him closely as I grew up under his wing (just as all kids watch and absorb from their parents). While he had his short-comings, like all parents do, integrity was a clear strength. The price did not matter to my dad.

Two situations are clearly chiseled in my memory and illustrate that integrity should not be for sale. We were going to build a table out of cedar and a neighbor, Mr. Derrick, had some cured cedar boards to sell. We went over in the pick-up and loaded the lumber. Dad said, "Mr. Derrick, how much do I owe you?" Mr. Derrick said, "Well Tom, I hear lumber is high now, I need $20 for this lumber." Dad grinned, said that would not be fair, that the fair price was $120, and handed Mr. Derrick the money. See, my dad was a builder and knew the price he paid was fair. As a lad of tender years, I was watching.

The companion event occurred when a man who owned a piece of property on the lake said, "Tom, I'm gonna sell that lot; will you give $8,000 for it?" Dad grinned and without hesitation said, "I'll give you $22,000 for it—that's what it's worth." Again, as a lad of twelve, I was watching.

Respecting Truth

Pilate, lacking integrity, lacked the ability to deal correctly with truth. We live today in a nation accustomed to the spin, spin control, and positions based on polls and surveys. Pilate, unable to do the right thing and unable to display integrity, finally said to Jesus, "What is truth?" (John 18:38) In the 1970s we called that "the ultimate cop-out."

Integrity understands, accepts and vigorously defends truth, facts and absolutes. Pilate was not interested in truth, but rather, in himself. Integrity and truth do not exist apart from each other. If you do not deal well with truth, you lack integrity.

In court when we swear witnesses in, we ask if they will tell the truth, the whole truth, and nothing but the truth. Can you be counted on to tell the whole truth? Do you make sure in your communications with others that you take responsibility and that you deliver the full and accurate message? Do you volunteer the whole truth?

Recently I presided over a jury trial involving complex property and property rights issues. The jury of twelve worked very hard, listened well and began split seven to five. After an additional day of deliberations, the vote was ten to two. It made it to eleven to one, and the jury was hung—no movement.

We then brought the jury out, and I explained that it was a "hung jury mistrial." The individual jurors were obviously weary and tense, and during their deliberations, we could even hear arguing coming from the jury room. Wanting to break the tension before we released them to go home, I thanked them for their service and told them that they were, in all my time as a judge, the wisest, hardest working and most focused jury that I had ever presided over. They each sat up straight, squared their shoulders, held their heads high, and smiled. After a pause to let them enjoy the compliment, I then told them the whole truth: not only were they the wisest, hardest working, and most focused jury I had ever had as a judge, but me being a new judge, also my very first and only jury! Telling the whole truth dissolved the jury into laughter and good will.

A refreshing example of the whole truth is always welcome in court and everyday life. A man came before me and pled guilty to "rolling through a stop sign." After accepting his guilty plea, I asked, "Is there anything you would like to say?" The gentleman replied in a clear deliberate voice, "Yes, Your Honor, I have been running that same stop sign every day for the past eight years and this is the first time they stopped me." The whole truth! Thank you, sir!

Do you have to be asked the perfect question in order to coax you to then tell the whole truth? Do you have to be pinned down to get it all out on the table? Integrity is eager to tell the whole truth.

Providing Security

Sadly, in our day integrity is too often lacking, but it is a welcome sight when found. Surrendering to the approval of others will thwart integrity. Integrity cannot be bought and is willing to deal with the truth in a straightforward fashion. Perhaps the greatest reward of integrity is security. Proverbs 10:9 says, "The man of integrity walks securely, but he who takes crooked paths will be found out." Integrity does not mind being "found out" because integrity has nothing to hide! Therefore, security rewards the man of integrity.

Everybody is watching, especially our children. Will you and I pass the test? Resolve, therefore, to be a person known for integrity.

Robert Duncan started working as a professional musician in Atlanta, Georgia. He toured as a keyboard player and background vocalist with Arista recording artist Paul Davis, during which time he also worked as songwriter for Webb IV Publishing. Later, after being baptized into Christ in Atlanta, Robert formed one of the first kingdom bands, Two Thirty Eight, and produced their debut album, *Know That We Care*. He played the role of the apostle John in the New York City Church of Christ's original version of the musical *UpsideDown* in 1987.

Robert moved to NYC in 1989, wrote music for *Sesame Street* and performed locally with his wife, Kim. In 1994, he began working for the Boston Church of Christ as director and producer of special events for the Boston church and the New England and Europe (NEEM) World Sector of the International Churches of Christ. He led DMI, a kingdom-based record label and produced, wrote and performed the music, along with his wife, for several albums. The Duncans currently live in New York with their six-year-old twins, son, Eli, and daughter, KJ, and their nine-year-old son, Joshua. Robert is currently working as a freelance producer of special events and music, and he and his wife have launched their new music publishing company, The North Corner Music Group (NCMG).

6 Simon the Sorcerer

Fame or Faith?

Robert Duncan

Peeking from behind the proscenium wall, Simon watched as the crowd of people continued spilling into the aisles. "Looks like another packed house tonight," whispered the stage manager as he pressed against Simon to get a better view of the auditorium. "Of course it's going to be packed, you idiot," scoffed Simon, pushing him away as he turned to the prop table to collect his array of costume and magic accessories. *It's all in the presentation,* Simon thought to himself as he methodically fastened his black and red cape around his neck, the silky, massive fabric cascading over his shoulders and around his back. "Standby—ten seconds," the stagehand relayed to the sorcerer. The auditorium suddenly fades to black. A lantern-generated "spotlight" shoots a wide circle of white light against the front center of the curtain. "Ladies and gentlemen!" barks the announcer standing off to the side of the stage apron, "We bring you the mystical, the magical, all-knowing, all-seeing, almighty…Simon the Sorcerer!"

Gripping the seams at the center of the proscenium curtain, Simon makes his dramatic entrance as he pulls the curtain apart, bursting into the pool of light. The audience leaps to their feet with a thunderous roar of applause and cheers. "Simon, you are so great!" shrieks a loyal fan. "I never miss one of Simon's events," a local political leader brags. "This man, Simon the Sorcerer *is* the divine power!" "Yes!" agrees someone standing near by, "He is so great, so talented!" "O-oh," coo the young girls as they fix their eyes on the caped magician, "He is so amazing! Simon is *the* Great Power!"

Simon the Sorcerer was the equivalent of a rock star. He was a first century superstar. He was Samaria's version of the Beatles,

N'Sync or Michael Jackson. Simon the Sorcerer's presentation of sorcery and magical illusions was like an hour and a half of one continual hit song after another, each magical trick followed by the frenzied, deafening response from the audience.

But Simon was way too impressed with himself. Fame. Glory. They intoxicate, medicate and eventually annihilate. Perhaps Simon the sorcerer needed a little boost to help his self-confidence. Maybe he had a vial of a narcotic substance tucked away until just before entering the stage. Or perhaps he kept a bottle of wine on the prop table that he would revisit between shows.

In Acts chapter 8, the Bible says that Simon amazed all the people of Samaria with his performances, his sorcery and his magic. Not only did they proclaim that he was great, but he proclaimed that he was great—he believed his own hype! Then one day Simon heard the good news of Jesus Christ, and the Bible said he believed. So far, so good. Later, the Bible says that Simon was "astonished by the great signs and miracles he saw" Philip doing (Acts 8:13). The dictionary defines the word "astonished" as "great amazement." This was the same kind of amazement that the crowds back in Samaria felt when they saw Simon's sorcery. His amazement is the first sign that maybe Simon was beginning to trade his belief back in for the attraction of performing.

When the apostles Peter and John arrive and decide to give the believers the gift of the Holy Spirit, Simon was immediately impressed. He might have thought, *This gift of the Holy Spirit might be just the thing that has been missing from my prop table. It would certainly enhance my performance.* Of course, Peter gave Simon a very intense rebuke: "You have no part or share in this ministry because your heart is not right before God" (Acts 8:21).

⟨₂⟩∞⟨₂⟩

Surely, Simon the Sorcerer must have found the praise and adoration of his loyal fans intoxicating. Every performer deep down inside really wants this. My dear fellow performers and artists, we have all dreamed and fantasized of one day drawing great crowds of people to see us perform. Every write-up, every article, every review about the most popular pop star, rock star, rap star, hip hop star, dancer, actor, director and writer—those of us who aspire to one day make a name for ourselves are all impressed by this, whether we admit it or not. Warning: It is dangerous to be too impressed by the world. It is even more dangerous to be too impressed with yourself.

Abundant Gifts

God blessed me with many artistic gifts. As a child, these gifts caught the attention of my parents. They tried to cultivate my talents as best they could. Making a little boy in the rural South take piano lessons is not exactly what little Southern boys want to do—certainly not something a Southern boy wants others to know about. However, taking lessons and performing are two different things.

I discovered I could use my talents to make friends. I could use them to acquire "bodyguards" in school. If you are not a big kid, you had best either make them laugh or impress them with your talent. I did both. But music is what impressed everyone the most. Going to school, doing the things that all the other kids did was okay as far as fitting in. But when I played piano, I was not just another kid on the playground. This was the beginning stage of equating my talent with my self-worth. I wonder if, as he was growing up, this is how little Simon got started. After all, it is obvious from the Scriptures that Simon the Sorcerer seemed unable to separate Simon the performer from Simon the man, Simon the disciple.

I am convinced that God has a purpose in mind when he blesses someone with special gifts and talents. Once God gives talent, he also gives the responsibility to cultivate it and manage it (Matthew 25:14–30). This is where our talents can go from being a blessing to a curse. It can become a curse when we take the talent God gives us and we abuse it. We forget that it came from God. The compliments pour over us and we begin to believe that these gifts are ours to claim and not gifts from God. We develop a dependence on compliments; without compliments we feel worthless.

Performing for the pure art of it or for the fulfillment of expression are both wonderful things. Performing to convey a feeling, a thought, a conviction or an experience takes it to a very different level—something that you have written or performed connects with someone in a very personal, profound way. In my pursuits as a songwriter and singer, the times that I have found most fulfilling were when I wrote songs from the heart, sang from the heart and connected emotionally with the audience. This is especially true when I have shared my music with an audience of disciples of Jesus Christ. The problem is when we as artists reach a point where the only way we can connect with other people emotionally is when we are performing.

Give or Take

Many artists are a study in contradiction. We are envied, we are applauded, we are praised, we are held up as being great, and yet we are some of the most insecure people on earth. So on the one hand, we are insecure. On the other hand, we are too easily impressed with ourselves, and when that happens, we stop relying on God.

I was baptized in 1986. Prior to my baptism I had worked for years as a musician, playing concerts and club gigs, working with a major recording artist and even appearing on *American Bandstand* and *Solid Gold*. On the outside, it looked as if I had arrived. But it was all a facade. My life was much like the sound stage for *American Bandstand*. On the TV screen, it looked like a huge room with two spiral stage risers and a huge studio audience that the cameraman would pan to from time to time. But backstage, as I watched the taping of the show preceding the one I was to appear on, I was surprised to see how small the sound stage really was. Those spiral risers were not that big at all. The audience was only a small cluster of young people clumped together in a little section of the room. Many things that impress us at first glance end up not being what they seem. Sadly, when

I look at the video of those taped TV appearances now, all I can think of is how high I was on cocaine as we were being broadcast around the world.

My life had been filled with the blessings of great, "natural" talent, combined with years of making bad decisions. The most consistent choice I made was drinking and getting high. When my substance abuse led to immorality, pregnancies and abortions, I always had a system for escaping the emotional pain. Drink another double shot of tequila and chase it with a couple of cold beers. The pain will go away. I had so many dreams as a young man, but because of my bad choices and my inability to cope with life, each of my dreams crashed and burned. I was convinced of impending success, only to realize later that it was not within my reach.

Road to Life

The year I turned thirty, the memories of shooting up heroin as a teenager were becoming more vivid and appealing to me. I always had the philosophy that to be at a point where you were willing to shoot up, you had to not care whether you lived or died. A syringe of warm heroin flowing through my veins seemed to be the most obvious choice of refuge for me in order to make the pain go away. I was truly at a crossroads, and I could feel the old familiar path that led to shooting up drugs calling me. That was when God made his move. He gave me just enough rope to hang myself, and then he reminded me that he loves me. This was when I met Sam Laing and began studying the Bible.

In 2 Samuel 22:36, David says, "You stoop down to make me great." God really did this for me. I was as down as a person could get. God stooped down and placed me in the path of disciples who wanted to help me understand the Bible in a way I had never understood it before. Yes, I stopped getting high. I saw my sin and saw how it had separated me from God. I was so happy to reach the point where I was ready to be baptized into Christ and become a disciple. I was ready to leave my life of sin in the past where it belonged.

However, my early years as a disciple were not easy. I had been a wild musician, obviously discipled by the world much longer than I had been discipled by the word of God. It was particularly challenging for those who were in my life trying to help me and to disciple me. But, thank God, they persevered! God *does* have a plan for us. During these past sixteen years as a disciple, God has proven he has a plan for me. And I have only lived out part of it so far!

Can't Run, Can't Hide

After being baptized in 1986 in Atlanta, I moved to New York City in 1989, taking my girlfriend, Kim Carter, with me. We joined the daytime ministry, with Kim sharing an apartment with sisters in Spanish Harlem while I moved in with brothers in Midtown. Two years later, we were married and moved to New Jersey. Then we had our first child, Joshua. In 1994, the Boston Church of Christ offered us a job and we accepted it. Living in a new city with a new job in a new church, leaving five years of relationships behind us, I found myself faced with more challenges than I thought I was ready for. So, I became a casual drinker, having a couple of beers every night.

I was in charge of producing special events in venues such as the Wang Theater, the Boston Garden, the Fleet Center and virtually every major facility in downtown Boston. Moreover, I was in charge of directing all the entertainment at the annual missions conferences in Paris, France. Kim became pregnant with twins. The pressure grew. I was finding relationships hard to build. More pressure. We were writing songs and producing CDs. But behind the scenes, Satan was creating jealousy and envy, driving a wedge between us and other disciples. More stress. And the more challenges that came, the more I began to drink. Five years later, my drinking had become so habitual that I knew deep inside that I might have a serious problem. Yes, I was in serious denial!

So, I would stop drinking—for a couple of days. Then I would start back. Ironically, one of my dearest friends, Willie Flores, was placed in charge of leading the new and improved Chemical

Recovery (CR) ministry for Boston. While friends of mine were among the first to join CR, I, in my pride refused to attend, claiming that I did not want to be another "high-profile" disciple to sign up.

Meanwhile, my personal life was becoming a nightmare. It got so bad that I did not have enough confidence to even lead a choir rehearsal unless I had had a couple of beers. I would sneak beer and bottles of wine into my basement office, being incredibly deceitful to my wife and children. I was in a trap with no way out. The only time I did not feel the stress of life and the pain of disappointments was when I would medicate by drinking.

I Wanna Be Set Free

Then one night I attended a CR graduation, and the sharing of a brother who was graduating moved me. The room was packed wall to wall, and here was this brother, oblivious to the hundreds of eyes that are watching him. Totally focused on his wife and children, this brother stood there sobbing, as he apologized for all the hurt and pain he had caused his wife and children. It was all I could do to keep from bursting out in tears. I thought, *How liberating that must feel! How much of a relief it must feel like to be able to stand there for all to see and freely weep, pouring your heart out, asking for forgiveness from your wife and children. Oh, how I needed that!*

Later that night, one thing continued to burn through my soul, one thing that I could no longer deny: I was an alcoholic. Turning to God and then to my wife, Kim, I decided to enter CR and do whatever it took to deal with this, even if it meant losing my job with the church.

> Some sat in darkness and the deepest gloom,
>   prisoners suffering in iron chains,
> for they had rebelled against the words of God
>   and despised the counsel of the Most High.
> So he subjected them to bitter labor;
>   they stumbled, and there was no one to help.

Then they cried to the LORD in their trouble,
    and he saved them from their distress.
He brought them out of darkness and the deepest gloom
    and broke away their chains. (Psalm 107:10 –14)

Run the Race

God brought me out of the deepest gloom, and he broke away the chains of alcoholism. On March 11, 2000, I stood in front of a packed house, not to perform, not to sing, but to look across the audience into the eyes of my wife and my son, Joshua, and tell them how sorry I was for all the hurt and pain that I had caused them. That night I graduated from CR.

This March I will celebrate my two-year anniversary of my graduation from CR. And it will mark three years since I had my last drink of alcohol. Am I cured? No. Am I still an alcoholic? Yes. And I will be "in recovery" for the rest of my life. If Simon the Sorcerer had only trusted God more than he had trusted himself, God could have brought him "out of darkness and the deepest gloom." If only Simon had relied on God for his strength instead of feeling the need to "perform," God would have surely broken away his chains. If only Simon had been humble, he would have realized what I had to realize, that whatever talents I have are by the grace of God, and ultimately, that God is the Great Power.

Michael B. Mount received a bachelor's degree in psychology and zoology in 1966 from the College of Wooster, in Wooster, Ohio; did postgraduate in work physiological psychology at DePauw University in Greencastle, Indiana; and obtained his juris doctorate degree in 1976 from the University of the Pacific, McGeorge School of Law, in Sacramento, California, after serving five years in the US Air Force during the Vietnam era. Currently he is general counsel for the San Francisco Church of Christ. He has recently taken on a similar role for the NET World Sector of the International Churches of Christ. He is also on the board of directors of HOPE *worldwide*, Northern California, Ltd., and Hope Technology Group.

Prior to moving to San Francisco to work for the church, Michael worked for the State Department of Developmental Services, a department within the California Health and Welfare Agency responsible for providing services to persons with developmental disabilities. For seven years he served as the department's chief counsel.

Michael has been a practicing attorney since 1976, with experience in both the public and private sector, including serving as an administrative hearing officer. He and his wife, Monnie, have a daughter, Amy. He became a disciple in 1994 in Sacramento.

7 Erastus

Man of Influence, Man of Sacrifice

Michael B. Mount

The day starts out early. Usually, he's there long before sunrise. There is much to do and meetings pack his schedule. The lamp still burns, but the sun is starting to shine through his window. The early hours are important to him—it is his chance to concentrate, get organized, plan out his day. Hopefully he can get some work done before everyone else shows up and things start to happen. Even though he is the boss, he has to answer to his boss and those higher up, his boss' bosses. But he thought, "What do they know? They couldn't find their way down to the waterworks if Zeus himself were here."

Who knows what crisis will come up today? No one ever notices all the days that the water runs fine or when the sewers don't back up. Storm clouds coming? Better check the viaducts. Governor coming unexpectedly? Make sure the streets are clean. Always on call, never appreciated.

Citizens line up outside his office with all sorts of complaints, demanding to see him. He can send them to see someone else, but he can't ignore them, even though he wants to sometimes. Deep inside he's reminded that the public is a force to be reckoned with when you are a civil servant. You serve at their pleasure. He also knows that if the powerful people, those who appointed him, don't like what he does, he could lose his job. This hangs over his head. He does not like it, but he knows that that's politics.

The hours fly by, the meetings are finished, and he realizes he forgot to eat his lunch. The day is almost over. He finally gets a chance to talk to some of the people who work for him, if he has not seen them or been involved with them during the day. It is starting to get dark. He lights the lamp. His desk is covered with all sorts of things he needs to read and review to be prepared for tomorrow, including the documents he never got to from the day before. He stays an hour or so longer, then decides to head home to be with his family, even though he's not done yet. He thinks, "I'll come in early tomorrow."

He reflects on his day and remembers feeling so overwhelmed at one point that he felt as if he was ready to explode from the pressure. He held it in today, but what about tomorrow? At the same time, he feels the lingering effects of the adrenaline that kept him stimulated and on the edge during the day. He thinks about the excitement of the challenges he faces, the fast pace, being in the battle and the feelings of power that come with being a "player" in such a high stakes game. He decides that the trade-off is acceptable, turns down the lamp and leaves with an arm full of papers, knowing that it all starts again tomorrow.

⟨⟩⟨⟩

Erastus was a first century government official about whom we know little. However, I believe he was included in the Bible because of who he was and what he sacrificed. As Jesus taught, "From everyone who has been given much, much will be demanded; and from the one who has been entrusted with much, much more will be asked" (Luke 12:48).

God recognized that forceful men would be needed to advance his kingdom (Matthew 11:12). God also knew that men like Erastus, men of many talents (Matthew 25:14–30), would be exposed to the gospel throughout the centuries and that powerful examples would be needed if such men were to be converted. In order to help us reach these individuals of influence, God gave us glimpses into their stories.

The Bible mentions Erastus three times:

> He [Paul] sent two of his helpers, Timothy and Erastus, to Macedonia, while he stayed in the province of Asia a little longer. (Acts 19:22)

> Erastus, who is the city's director of public works, and our brother Quartus send you their greetings. (Romans 16:23)

> Erastus stayed in Corinth, and I left Trophimus sick in Miletus. (2 Timothy 4:20)

Although we can only speculate about Erastus and his life, the Scriptures and our knowledge of the times provide some helpful insights. Paul wrote his letter to the church in Rome during his last visit to Corinth. The personal greetings at the end of the letter, which include a reference to Erastus, are from members of the Corinthian church to their brothers and sisters in Rome. So we know Erastus was a Christian in the Corinthian church.

The NIV states that Erastus was "the city's director of public works." The word used in the Greek New Testament is *oikonomos,* which refers generally to a manger, but was sometimes used to describe a treasurer or other government official. Whatever his actual position, Erastus was a civil servant of some type and a man of prominence.

At the time, Corinth was a major city and the center of a Roman province. Erastus' job description would likely have included the role of an administrator. He almost certainly would have supervised a large staff, of which he had the authority to hire and fire. He probably delegated the more menial tasks, while he oversaw implementation and completion of the works. As in most bureaucracies, he surely would have had to fight for his budget, competing with other agencies or departments for a share of the available funding. Since funding is typically allocated to what the people and the bureaucrats believe are the most important and critical functions, he may even have had to contact his political friends in Corinth to use their influence in helping him to secure what he needed.

We can be confident that he was a man of action, someone who could handle pressure. His day would have been busy and very demanding, with many people seeking his input. He would be called on to make decisions, and the decisions he made would affect many. He would have needed to be a quick thinker, decisive, assertive, bold, confident, willing to listen, a good negotiator, patient and self-disciplined. No matter how things went, he would ultimately be held responsible and accountable for the result.

Because he held such a position of importance, he was most likely a Roman citizen and a Gentile. As was typically the case, he either came from a prominent family or married into one and was probably well educated. He very likely would have been an influential, powerful and wealthy man, a man of property and possessions. We do not know his age, but he was probably an older man. Unless he was a rare Gentile, any religious practices he engaged in, prior to being converted, would have been pagan.

Despite all that Erastus had, we know that it did not fulfill him spiritually or minister to his heart, because he ultimately gave it all up. We do not know where or by whom he was converted, but it is likely that Paul converted him during one of his visits to Corinth. Because of his position and status as a Roman citizen, Erastus may have been unwilling to listen to anyone other than another citizen of Rome, like Paul. Whatever happened, God moved in his heart in a dramatic way and he not only became a believer, but a trusted servant. The Scriptures tell us that he was a brother in Christ and one of Paul's helpers. So, we know he was taught the gospel and God's expectation of sacrifice and surrender. Paul apparently had high regard for Erastus because Paul sent him with Timothy to Macedonia to preach the word and to prepare the way for him. He would not have given such an important mission to or entrusted Timothy to someone untrustworthy. Obviously, Erastus was a reliable man.

Although the reference to Macedonia makes it clear that Erastus had left Corinth to be part of the early missionary ministry, we do not know how long he was gone or whether he ever returned to his position of prominence. It is doubtful. The last mention of Erastus in the Scriptures places him back in Corinth during the time Paul was a prisoner in Rome. Given his desire to do God's will, he probably returned and stayed, at Paul's request, to help grow and strengthen the Corinthian church. The city had a reputation as a place of wickedness, so the church needed strong leaders.

We can only guess, but he may have become an overseer (a deacon or an elder) in the church. (See Acts 20:28.) This would have been the role that a trustworthy and talented follower such as he might have been given. If he served in the church, we can be sure that his life of comfort and privilege had ended. As a disciple of Christ, he was undoubtedly experiencing hardship, persecution and austere times (2 Corinthians 6:3–10; 2 Timothy 3:12; 1 Peter 4:12–19). What a very different existence from the life he led as a government official for Corinth.

Like Erastus, I was also a government official at the time I became a disciple. I was chief counsel for the Department of Developmental Services for the state of California and part of the agency's executive staff. This department oversees the provision of services for the developmentally disabled in California. In my role I had frequent interactions with legislative staff and members of the governor's office staff. I was used to dealing with people of authority and prominence, providing advice to them and making legal recommendations that had the potential to influence many lives.

Out of the World, into Christ

About a year and a half before my own conversion, my wife and daughter had become disciples. I was still holding out, only going to service with them on special occasions. The department was involved in some very complex litigation during that time and as lead counsel, I was working very long hours. I had very little time off, even on the weekends. I used all these as excuses for not studying the Bible. When the litigation finally settled, I ran out of excuses. Though I was half-hearted at first, I eventually learned about my sinful nature and how my sin, especially my pride and selfish ambition, had affected my marriage, my daughter and my other relationships. But I also heard the good news: Despite all these shortcomings and sins, God not only loved me but Christ died for me. Two months after I started studying the

Bible, I was baptized. Then, two months later, my ninety-four-year-old mother also became a disciple.

Trust Through Trials

I do not think I really felt the full impact of my commitment to Christ (Luke 9:23–26) until I was asked by church leaders to resign from my position with the state and move to San Francisco because of needs there. Since my baptism, I had thought that I was ready to go anywhere and do anything for God—and had said so many times. However, when it came time to respond to God's new vision for my life, my faith was seriously tested. We were being asked to move to San Francisco, an area where the cost of living was among the highest in the country. My wife and I would need to look for new jobs, sell our home and relocate our family, including my mother. This meant finding a place for us to live and a suitable nursing home nearby for her.

At the time I was fifty-five years old, and I was not sure what the job market would be like, especially for someone who had spent the previous eighteen years in public service. So, I contacted all the people I could think of who could help me find another civil service job. Some of them were former colleagues at the governor's office and the office of the attorney general. I also had sent more than thirty resumes out to state agencies, city attorneys and county counsel in the San Francisco area. I was looking for a sign of some sort, and I tied everything to the job market. Yet nothing positive was turning up. Either there were no openings, or I was at the top of the selection list but the agency was in a hiring freeze, or I was overqualified.

With each rejection, my faith took a hit. My confidence was shaken. My pride was exposed. I became more anxious and impatient, and I began to become discouraged. I could not understand why someone with my experience and contacts was having such a difficult time. What would I say to my friends and coworkers? What would I say to my family and my wife's family? I started to doubt and to question whether this was really God's will for my life.

God's Control

Yet all along, I had been praying that God would reveal his plan for me by the week of November first, the day my resignation would be announced at the agency. A week or so before that date, I got a call to tell me that Russ Ewell, lead evangelist for the San Francisco Church of Christ, wanted to meet with me the weekend of November first. At our meeting, God's plan became clear when Russ offered me a job to do legal work for the church and to help develop and expand the operations of the Hope Technology Group. Now I understood why none of the other job opportunities had worked out. God knew all along his plan for me. He had given me a sign by closing the doors to the civil service jobs, but I could not see it. I had been living by sight, not faith—the exact opposite of what God expects (2 Corinthians 5:7). These challenges taught me a lot about not doubting (James 1:6–8) and the importance of staying faithful no matter what may be going on (or not going on) around me (Romans 4:18–21).

Although I quickly made the decision to work for the church, I finally understood what it meant to be asked to give up everything for Christ (Luke 14:26–33). The sacrifices and self-denial that had occurred in my life up to that time had worked on my character, but they were all things I had been willing to accept or were "manageable" and within my zone of comfort. I had not been tested this deeply before. Position, job security, retirement, the comforts of the world, my home—all became larger than life to me. Moreover, my testing was not concluded just because I had a job to go to in San Francisco. God exposed more of my character as the realities of my decision began to set in.

Character Refinement

I started seeing the real financial impact. I realized the amount of retirement money I would lose as a result of resigning my position and retiring early. I was trying to sell our home in a depressed market. We would have to pay rent at a rate higher than my previous mortgage payment. My wife would need to find a teaching position that would provide the extra income we would need to live on. The stress of these issues began to hit home, and I did not deal with them like I should.

I am not one who typically has fits of rage, but I had two such outbursts fairly close together, both related to financial pressure. I had never realized how much the safety and security of my retirement account meant to me. It was my pot of gold at the end of the rainbow. God was now exposing the secret sin of my heart: greed. I was the rich fool that Jesus described in Luke 12:13–21. Fortunately, through much counsel and prayer, I was able to make the decision that the man in Jesus' story failed to make.

Once again, God blessed us. We found a great place to live, with a wonderful nursing home seven miles away. We sold our home within four days of putting it on the market. My wife was able to start substitute teaching almost immediately after we moved, and my former agency asked me to continue to work for them as a litigation consultant for several months after retirement. This gave us some additional income during the transition period. God more than met all our needs (Philippians 4:19).

Living Out God's Dreams

I am so thankful for my wife and daughter and the other disciples who helped me to see that this was about God and his plan, not mine (Jeremiah 10:23; Proverbs 14:11–12, 15:22, 16:9, 18:17, 21:2). Since coming to San Francisco, God has blessed us in many ways, including allowing me to use my twenty-five years of legal experience to serve the church and the NET World Sector.[1] Who but God would have had a vision for how my background working with the developmentally disabled, and my wife's experience as a special education teacher, could be used for such an awesome purpose? We have served in the church's Spiritual Resources ministry, helping children with special needs, and I oversee the legal aspects of the program. I have also had the opportunity to provide advice on various special-education related issues to the parents of many of the children we serve through our parent support groups. This has been deeply rewarding.

Perhaps the greatest blessing has been our involvement with the Hope Technology School, a full inclusion school for typical and special needs children, run by a separate nonprofit organization. I serve as president of the board of directors, my daughter is a teacher at the school and my wife is a volunteer classroom aid. Together, we have the opportunity to work with the dedicated professionals at the school who love and care for these special children. It is truly amazing to be able to use the gifts God has given us in this way. Without doubt, we have received much more than we ever gave up (Luke 18:29–30). God has opened our eyes to see what a great impact this ministry can have throughout the kingdom and we feel blessed to be a small part of it.

One of the main lessons from the life of Erastus is that all lost people are reachable, no matter who they are or what position they hold. I am eternally grateful for the disciples who reached out to my family and me.

How About You?

So where is your level of faith right now? Who are you intimidated to share your faith with? So often we meet someone at work or during other parts of our day, and depending on who they are or what they do, we may be afraid to reach out to them. We hesitate to share our faith and our lives. We become fearful of what they may think, especially if they are a coworker, our boss or a person of influence and authority. We look at their lives, what they have, and doubt that we can convert them. Often they seem happier and more "together" than we do, and we question whether they would be willing to give up what they have to become a disciple. We forget the lessons from our past, how we tried to hide what was really going on in our lives and how Christ rescued us from all this.

Think of Erastus and the disciples who reached out to him. Undoubtedly there was some fear as they shared the gospel with him, not knowing what might happen to them. However, this did not stop them from loving him (1 John 4:18) and seeing him for who he really was: a lost soul. They were about Jesus' purpose

(Luke 19:10). Because of their courage and love, Erastus is our brother in Christ. To whom do you need to reach out?

Be bold (Psalm 138:3; Acts 4:29, 9:28). Have a willingness to sacrifice your dreams and security for God's dreams (Matthew 6:26–33). Then watch God use your life to convert the next Erastus!

Note

[1]See footnote on page 50.

Robert H. Wilkins was born and reared in Pittsburgh, Pennsylvania. He received bachelor's degree in 1955 and his MD in 1959 from the University of Pittsburgh. In 1957, Bob was married to Gloria Ann Kohl, who also is a Pitt graduate. They have three children and three grandchildren.

Bob's residency training included two years in general surgery and five years in neurosurgery at the Duke University Medical Center in Durham, North Carolina, separated by two years in the Surgery Branch of the National Cancer Institute in Bethesda, Maryland. After concluding his residency, Bob served sequentially as assistant professor of neurosurgery at Duke (1968–72), chairman of the Department of Neurosurgery at the Scott and White Clinic in Temple, Texas (1972–75), associate professor of neurosurgery at Pitt (1975–76), professor and chief of the Division of Neurosurgery at Duke (1976–96), and professor of neurosurgery at Duke (1996–present).

Bob has been active in a number of neurosurgical, surgical and medical organizations. He has published more than 300 medical papers and book chapters, has edited or written twenty-eight books on neurosurgical subjects, and has served as editor or member of the editorial board of seven neurosurgical journals.

Of far greater importance for Bob, he has been a disciple at the Triangle church since June 29, 2000.

8 Apollos

Let Not the Wise Man Boast of His Wisdom

Robert H. Wilkins

A pollos was a Jew from Alexandria, Egypt. We first hear about him in the Bible after he had come to Ephesus, a city in the western part of Asia Minor that now forms part of Turkey. For centuries before Apollos, starting in about 665 BC, the Greeks had played an increasingly important role in Egypt. The city of Alexandria was founded by Alexander the Great in 331 BC. Following Alexander's death, one of his generals, Ptolemy, proclaimed himself king of Egypt in 305 BC and declared Alexandria the royal capital. In 295 BC, Ptolemy established an important center of learning there, with an associated library which eventually housed the original or a copy of most of the works that comprised the world's literature. Some of this fabulous collection was destroyed by fire in 48 BC and would not have been available to Apollos. However, he probably was influenced by the strong emphasis on learning that existed in Alexandria as he was growing up, during or shortly after the time when Jesus was on earth.

Apollos was an educated and eager man, but initially was somewhat off the mark as a disciple of Jesus. Luke describes an important encounter he had in Ephesus and gives us several insights into his life.

> Meanwhile a Jew named Apollos, a native of Alexandria, came to Ephesus. He was a learned man, with a thorough knowledge of the Scriptures. He had been instructed in the way of the Lord, and he spoke with great fervor and taught about Jesus accurately, though he knew only the baptism of John. He began to speak boldly in the synagogue. When Priscilla and Aquila heard him, they invited him to their home and explained to him the way of God more adequately.

> When Apollos wanted to go to Achaia, the brothers encour-
> aged him and wrote to the disciples there to welcome him. On
> arriving, he was a great help to those who by grace had believed.
> For he vigorously refuted the Jews in public debate, proving from
> the Scriptures that Jesus was the Christ. (Acts 18:24 –28)

Later when Paul came to Ephesus, he found the problem that
Apollos' teaching had created. Again, Luke describes it for us:

> While Apollos was at Corinth, Paul took the road through the
> interior and arrived at Ephesus. There he found some disciples and
> asked them, "Did you receive the Holy Spirit when you believed?"
> They answered, "No, we have not even heard that there is a
> Holy Spirit."
> So Paul asked, "Then what baptism did you receive?"
> "John's baptism," they replied.
> Paul said, "John's baptism was a baptism of repentance. He
> told the people to believe in the one coming after him, that is, in
> Jesus." On hearing this, they were baptized into the name of the
> Lord Jesus. When Paul placed his hands on them, the Holy Spirit
> came on them, and they spoke in tongues and prophesied. There
> were about twelve men in all. (Acts: 19:1 –7)

After leaving Ephesus, Apollos proved to be a powerful, even
divisive, force in the budding church in Corinth. The latter almost
certainly was not intentional on his part, but was simply a man-
ifestation of his considerable influence over his Christian brothers. However, it left Paul with the challenge of unifying the
Corinthian disciples, without eradicating the possible future
value of Apollos to the growth of the Christian movement. In his
first letter to the church in Corinth, Paul addressed the discord in
the following way:

> I appeal to you, brothers, in the name of our Lord Jesus Christ,
> that all of you agree with one another so that there may be no
> divisions among you and that you may be perfectly united in mind
> and thought. My brothers, some from Chloe's household have
> informed me that there are quarrels among you. What I mean is
> this: One of you says, "I follow Paul"; another, "I follow Apollos";
> another, "I follow Cephas"; still another, "I follow Christ."

> Is Christ divided? Was Paul crucified for you? Were you bap-
> tized into the name of Paul? For Christ did not send me to baptize,
> but to preach the gospel—not with words of human wisdom, lest the
> cross of Christ be emptied of its power. (1 Corinthians 1:10 -13, 17)

> You are still worldly. For since there is jealousy and quarreling
> among you, are you not worldly? Are you not acting like mere
> men? For when one says, "I follow Paul," and another, "I follow
> Apollos," are you not mere men?
> What, after all, is Apollos? And what is Paul? Only servants,
> through whom you came to believe—as the Lord has assigned to
> each his task. I planted the seed, Apollos watered it, but God made
> it grow. So neither he who plants nor he who waters is anything, but
> only God, who makes things grow. (1 Corinthians 3:3 -7)

In the same letter, Paul also placed emphasis on the necessi-
ty of man's humility in learning, understanding and teaching
God's word. Perhaps this was especially included for the benefit
of Apollos:

> When I came to you, brothers, I did not come with eloquence or
> superior wisdom as I proclaimed to you the testimony about God.
> For I resolved to know nothing while I was with you except Jesus
> Christ and him crucified. I came to you in weakness and fear, and
> with much trembling. My message and my preaching were not
> with wise and persuasive words, but with a demonstration of the
> Spirit's power, so that your faith might not rest on men's wisdom,
> but on God's power. (1 Corinthians 2:1 -5)

> Do not deceive yourselves. If any one of you thinks he is wise by the
> standards of this age, he should become a "fool" so that he may
> become wise. For the wisdom of this world is foolishness in God's
> sight. As it is written: "He catches the wise in their craftiness"; and
> again, "The Lord knows that the thoughts of the wise are futile."
> So then, no more boasting about men! All things are yours,
> whether Paul or Apollos or Cephas or the world or life or death
> or the present or the future—all are yours, and you are of Christ,
> and Christ is of God. (1 Corinthians 3:18 -23)

The exact role of Apollos in the early development of Christianity is uncertain. Initially at least, there were flaws in his doctrine. In Corinth, Apollos probably influenced the church members with his erudition and oratorical talents, and some came to view him as a rival of Paul rather than as Paul's successor. However, the commendation of him in one of Paul's last letters (Titus 3:13) would make it appear that Apollos learned from Priscilla, Aquila and others and went on to use his considerable skills for the good of the kingdom. It is even believed by some scholars that he may very well been the author of Hebrews.

I have recently retired from the practice of neurosurgery, but I have retained the position of professor of neurosurgery at the Duke University Medical Center and continue to teach the neurosurgical residents at that institution on a weekly basis. Throughout my career as an academic neurosurgeon, my greatest joy has come from learning and teaching.

Making 'Disciples'

From 1976 to 1996 (before I became a Christian), I served as chief of the Duke Division of Neurosurgery. In that capacity I was instrumental in recruiting an outstanding Duke medical student, Estrada Bernard, into our residency program for seven years of training, 1983 to 1990. I told him that he would have to be totally committed to his profession, that he would be expected to work day and night, and that he would be paid relatively little money during his residency. I also told him that if he performed in a satisfactory manner and didn't make any serious mistakes, he would be likely to have a successful thirty year (or more) career as a neurosurgeon after his residency. So far, Estrada has followed these guidelines exactly, and he now is chief of the Division of Neurosurgery at the University of North Carolina. I would later learn that Estrada, during his extremely busy and stressful year as chief resident in 1989–1990, was baptized and became a disciple at the Triangle Church of Christ. His physician wife, Cora, also became a disciple.

In 1995, I was instrumental in recruiting to our faculty an excellent Yale-trained neurosurgeon, Timothy George, who was in the second year of a pediatric neurosurgery fellowship in Chicago. I gave Tim the exact same guidelines and vision that I had shared with Estrada. I believed he could have a successful career as a pediatric neurosurgeon. So far, Tim has followed these guidelines exactly, and he is a valued faculty member of the Duke Division of Neurosurgery. Soon after Tim and his wife, Rosalind, arrived in Durham, Estrada and Cora invited them to church and eventually both became disciples at the Triangle Church of Christ.

My wife, Gloria, and I came to know and love Estrada, Cora, Tim and Rosalind through our professional ties. They began to invite us to church in 1999, and we were touched by what we encountered.

Case History

I must digress here, to supply some background information about my previous spiritual life. When I was growing up, I attended church regularly with my parents, sang in the church choir, and attended the church's camp each summer. Yet I absorbed very little from the Scriptures, and after my teen years I seldom attended church. Through my family, I had developed sound moral values and a strong sense of right and wrong. Subsequently, during my career as a neurosurgeon, I considered myself an accomplished professional who helped people deal with their medical problems. I felt satisfied that I was living as I should—and presumably as God wanted me to live.

From Teacher to Student

In the spring of 2000, I began a series of personal Bible studies with disciples from the Triangle Church—Arthur Grayson, leader of the Arts and Medical Ministry, and physicians Kevin Broyles, Bill Thompson (who subsequently became my close friend and discipler) and Tim George. Those studies brought home to me how self-directed and selfish my life had been and how I needed to change to take advantage of the opportunity that had been provided to me by God through the death and resurrection of his Son, Jesus Christ. In recruiting terms, I found out that I would need to be totally committed to God, that I would be expected to work at this day and night, and that I would not be paid money for this effort, but instead would be expected to tithe. However, if I made mistakes but continued to seek God's direction in my life, these events would be forgiven, and if I tried to the best of my ability to emulate Jesus, I would be rewarded with eternal life in heaven. I was baptized on June 29, 2000.

Before my conversion, my circumstances were different from Apollos' in that I did not have extensive knowledge of the Bible and did not try to influence others from a religious point of view. However, I was knowledgeable in other areas and did exert an influence on people because of this. Like Apollos, I needed to learn God's truth. Both Apollos and I had to become humble in order to learn, which may have been harder for Apollos because he already had extensive religious knowledge. For me, it required a reversal of roles. I had to go from begin a teacher to being a student. I had taught Estrada Bernard and supervised Tim George, but as I became their pupil, I discovered how much each of them could teach me about things far more important than neurosurgery.

Life-Threatening Pride

Doctors in general, and surgeons in particular, tend to be proud of their knowledge and accomplishments. What they do professionally literally affects the lives of their patients. Unfortunately, a doctor may inflate a sense of authority into a feeling of arrogant self-importance, bordering on omnipotence. Satisfaction with a job done well becomes a sinful pride, which interferes with interpersonal relationships and more importantly, with a relationship with God. The physician having such an exaggerated view of his or her role in the practice of medicine would do well to remember the words of the famous surgeon Ambroise Paré (1510–1590), who put the emphasis in the proper place: "I dressed him and God healed him."

Furthermore, it is easy for a physician to become so engrossed in his or her demanding career that the career becomes the first priority, often to the detriment of the physician's relationships with spouse and children. The doctor needs to avoid becoming "married" to the career at the expense of his or her own family.

Prescription: Humility and Truth

In order to learn anything, an individual needs to recognize that he or she does not know everything about the subject and has something to learn. He or she needs a willingness to learn, to change opinions, to alter beliefs and to be taught, even by a younger person. In order to learn and understand the word of God, to act on it and to teach it, the individual needs to become humble and accepting. This approach is stated succinctly in Proverbs 11:2, "When pride comes, then comes disgrace, but with humility comes wisdom." The individual needs to have a genuine love for God and for truth and needs to overcome the selfish pride that presents a barrier to the process.

The knowledge possessed by humans is incomplete, and often enough is partially or totally erroneous. In contrast, God's word is absolute and timeless. As Jesus stated when he was praying for his disciples, "Sanctify them by the truth; your word is truth" (John 17:17). And Paul wrote in his letter to the Colossians,

> See to it that no one takes you captive through hollow and decep-
> tive philosophy, which depends on human tradition and the basic
> principles of this world rather than on Christ. (Colossians 2:8)

Spiritual Health

For me, the take-home messages from a review of the life of Apollos and my own conversion are these:

1. No matter where each of us is in our individual growth as a Christian, we always have more to learn and more to achieve spiritually. We must constantly strive to seek God's truth, while placing less emphasis on human knowledge and values. To facilitate this process, we must reduce the barriers that we ourselves create through our selfishness and pride.

We must become humble and receptive in order to really absorb—and then teach correctly—the word of God. As exemplified by the instruction of Apollos by Priscilla and Aquila, such teaching can have an exponential effect, as a pupil in turn becomes a teacher of others.

2. Knowledgeable individuals who are skilled in speaking and writing exert an influence that is magnified by such skills. Therefore, a person with these talents needs to be especially careful to teach God's word accurately.

3. As Paul pointed out, God has endowed each disciple with unique gifts (Romans 12:4–8; 1 Corinthians 12:12–31). Yet each disciple is a part of a larger body—the very body of Christ—and each should use his or her talents for the benefit of the whole. We must have unity among the disparate members so that the church can fulfill God's purpose effectively. God will work through the disciples who take the lead and also through those who support and follow those who lead.

4. Finally, as disciples of Jesus Christ, we need to follow Paul's advice to Timothy, "Watch your life and doctrine closely. Persevere in them, because if you do, you will save both yourself and your hearers" (1 Timothy 4:16).

Part 2

Themes

Randy Jordan is the husband of Jan and father of Mandy and Rob. He currently serves as the world sector administrator and general counsel for the international faith-based charity, HOPE *worldwide*. In addition, Randy serves as a congregational elder in the Greater Philadelphia Church of Christ.

Randy holds a bachelor's degree in pharmacy from the University of Florida, a master's degree in public administration and juris doctorate from Florida State University. In 1977, Randy established the Colonial Drug Store, a retail pharmacy in Reddick, Florida, and operated the pharmacy until being admitted to law school in 1981. After law school, he joined the health-care law firm of Epstein, Becker & Green, PC, and became a partner in 1994.

Randy has spoken on numerous national programs on the topic of health care and insurance regulation and authored the first edition of the portfolio entitled "Regulation of Provider Risk Sharing and Other Limitations on Risk Bearing Provider Networks," which was published as part of BNA's *Health Law and Business* series. Randy became a disciple in 1972 in Gainesville, Florida.

9 Marriage and Family

Priorities of a Professional

Randy Jordan

During my first semester of law school, I met Bill, a single Jewish man who was willing to befriend me as a slightly older, married law student with two small children. I remember reflecting on the academic advantage that Bill had because he did not have to split his time between school and family responsibilities. I will even admit to having a little jealousy as I saw Bill log hours of study time in preparation for exams, while I had to concern myself with the needs of a wife, daughter and son. I acknowledged in my mind that family commitments were important for a Christian husband and father, but my ambition to succeed in law school carved out room in my heart for the belief that family life was burdensome.

One evening I invited Bill to our home for a spaghetti dinner. As the conversation moved from topic to topic, Bill commented on how great it was to be in a family setting. Pushing the subject further, he stated that I was fortunate to have my family to come home to each day. Bill confessed that law school was his only focus and that he feared that he was becoming isolated from "real life." Finally, as I sat in convicted astonishment, Bill admonished me to never take my family for granted and to always be thankful for the balance to life provided by my wife and children. Few conversations have taught me more about the importance of maintaining God's priorities on marriage and family, and I am forever grateful to my friend.

Perspectives and Priorities

In a more recent conversation with John Partington, a fellow elder, I was being open about the internal pressure that I sometimes feel because of the battle between my commitment to work and to my family. John pointed me to the early chapters of the book of Genesis and showed me that this problem has been around from the beginning of time. His brief history lesson gave me another new insight about God's views of work and marriage.

In Genesis 2, God addressed Adam's need for friendship by saying, "It is not good for man to be alone, I will make a helper suitable for him" (v18). Then, God miraculously created a new human being out of Adam's rib, calling her "'woman,' for she was taken out of man" (v23). To complete the union, God proclaimed that these two distinct people would "become one flesh" (v24) as husband and wife. The Garden of Eden became the home of the first marriage.

Sadly, we find in Genesis 3 that sin made its way into the world to destroy Eden when Adam and Eve ate of the forbidden fruit. We learn that God's sense of justice demanded that the first sinners pay a price. God explained Adam's curse by saying:

> To Adam he said, "Because you listened to your wife and ate from the tree about which I commanded you, 'You must not eat of it,'
> "Cursed is the ground because of you;
>   through painful toil you will eat of it
>   all the days of your life.
> It will produce thorns and thistles for you,
>   and you will eat the plants of the field.
> By the sweat of your brow
>   you will eat your food
> until you return to the ground,
>   since from it you were taken;
> for dust you are
>   and to dust you will return." (Genesis 3:17–19)

As one who loves work and considers it a blessing, I was shocked by the realization that God had used work as a means of punishing Adam for violating the sacred terms of life in the Garden of Eden. Indeed, work was part of the curse that God applied to the ground, forever changing the dynamic of marriage for Adam and Eve.

When God set the original priorities for man and woman in the Garden of Eden, clearly the marriage relationship was second only to man's relationship with God himself. As the consequences of his sin, Adam now had to divert his attention to toiling in the fields to provide for his family, instead of focusing his full attention and desires on Eve, in accordance with God's original design. When we let our commitment to work invade either one of these top two priorities, we too are succumbing to Adam's curse. Clearly, God expects Christians to be diligent and responsible workers, but work must exist within a godly context, and the Bible tells us in Hebrews 13:4 that "marriage should be honored by all."

Growing As a Couple

I have never been completely comfortable with the extra degree of respect that is afforded those who attain professional status. My parents taught me that everyone puts their pants on one leg at a time. However, I have come to accept that higher levels of education and job titles do communicate something about a person's potential to make a difference. I have seen this phenomenon sometimes transfer subtly to relationships within the church.

In my case, I practiced pharmacy for five years before entering law school and have worked as a lawyer for the past seventeen years. As I achieved some modicum of success professionally, I found that others would seek me out to serve on professional and community boards. Even in the church, I seemed to be called upon for public speaking and various leadership roles with increasing frequency. Frankly, it was gratifying to find that I might have something to offer that was considered valuable by others.

My wife, Jan, on the other hand, assisted me in the operation of our pharmacy in the early years of our marriage. Although she had graduated with an elementary education major, she chose to pursue motherhood rather than seek employment in her chosen profession of teaching. Jan is a gifted woman with many talents, but it became apparent to her over time that her opportunities to serve were not as many as mine. Even in the church, there became a disparity between Jan's leadership role and mine. Subtly, her personal confidence began to erode, and she started questioning our compatibility as a married couple. To my shame, I was oblivious to her concerns—after all, everything was going great for me.

One day during a particularly painful discussion, Jan shared with me that she sometimes wondered whether I would have been better off marrying someone else. She wondered whether she was holding me back. I was afraid and embarrassed at the same time: afraid that my wife was experiencing so much insecurity and unhappiness, and embarrassed that I was so unaware and insensitive. Such is the plight of a selfishly ambitious married professional.

I realized on that day that I had led our marriage under a flawed assumption. I assumed that Jan shared equally in any victories that I experienced. Looking back, I can see clearly that I had observed only half of the instruction in Ephesians 5:28 for husbands to "love their wives as their own bodies." I had loved myself, but in my drive to succeed, I was blinded to my wife's need for personal victory stories and benchmarks of success. I committed to Jan that from that moment forward, I would only go places from a leadership perspective where we could go together. Slowly, Jan's self confidence returned and our relationship began to grow in new and exciting ways. Ironically, I found that I began to achieve a greater sense of accomplishment from her successes than from mine.

Four years ago, we took the principle of growing together to a new level when I resigned my law firm partnership so that she and I could work together at the faith-based charity, HOPE *worldwide*. Today, we also have the privilege of serving as elder and wife for the Greater Philadelphia Church of Christ. It is a glorious partnership that we now share, but we would not be where we are today without my having made the decision that we would grow together.

Respect One Another

One of the most penetrating questions that can be asked of a husband or wife by his or her spouse is, "Do you respect me?"

Husbands are offered some advantage on this topic by the Scriptures when Paul instructs in Ephesians 5:33 that "the wife must respect her husband." Wives are not ignored, however, when husbands, in 1 Peter 3:7, are encouraged to "be considerate" of their wives and "treat them with respect." Nevertheless, true respect between spouses is often elusive, particularly when one or both spouses are professionals.

For professionals working in their area of expertise, respect is assumed. By definition, professionals have specialized skills and abilities that are not common to most men and women. We are trained to gain confidence in our abilities, because others are wholly reliant upon our competence. Our credentials are intended to support the notion that our advice is worthy of respect.

Interestingly, no matter how married professionals are viewed in the work setting, they go home every evening to a place where respect must be built, not on credentials, but on service to others. In the prelude to the most extensive discussion of the marriage relationship in the Bible, the apostle Paul encourages Christians to "submit to one another out of reverence for Christ" (Ephesians 5:21). What follows is a challenging discussion by Paul of how the marriage relationship should be like the relationship between Christ and the church. Wives are charged with submitting to their husbands "as the church submits to Christ," and husbands are commanded to love their wives, "just as Christ loved the church and gave himself up for her" (Ephesians 5:24–25). Admittedly, the degree of love and respect that is required in order to serve at this level is no easy task for married couples under the best of circumstances; but when a touch of "professional" pride is added, it can seem nearly impossible.

I find that the issue of disrespect expresses itself in my marriage in three ways. First, and probably foremost, is failing to seek and trust in my wife's opinion. Although I have grown accustomed as a disciple to seeking advice from others, at heart I am an independent thinker. I sometimes find it inefficient to include others in decision making, particularly if I think that their input is unnecessary. If you are beginning to sense a hint of arrogance in this approach, I have to plead guilty as charged. In marriage, however, I have discovered that more than just poor decision making occurs with this degree of independent thinking: separation and distance result. When I have excluded Jan from decision making, I send the message that I do not really value her thoughts and ideas. However, as we have grown in our openness with one another, I have made an amazing discovery. I have found that my most trusted advisor and confidant is my wife. Although her analytic skills may not have been honed by the Socratic method and she may not have been trained on legal advocacy techniques, she knows me better than anyone and offers the best advice.

A second source of disrespect is the failure to be courteous. As a lawyer, I have been trained in the "adversarial system of justice." The theory behind this approach is that if both sides aggressively argue their case, somehow justice and truth will prevail. All I can say is that what works in the courtroom rarely works in the bedroom—or any other room in my house for that matter. In all seriousness, rude behavior, harsh comments, terse answers and thoughtless criticisms have no place in a marriage. Such conduct should be replaced by the admonition of the apostle Paul to

> ...not let any unwholesome talk come out of your mouths, but only
> what is helpful for building others up according to their needs,
> that it may benefit those who listen. (Ephesians 4:29)

The final area in which I am prone to show disrespect in my marriage is in not sharing my personal schedule. The busy-ness of professional life is challenging. Long work hours, extra business meetings and frequent travel put pressure on the personal schedules of married couples and their children. Under these circumstances, the coordination of schedules among family members will not happen without proper planning and communication. I always know that I have failed in this area when Jan says something like, "You are going to Los Angeles next week? I didn't know." Or "You didn't tell me that Steve and Theresa were coming over on Monday." I used to blame these scheduling oversights on being absent-minded, but I have learned that it is a matter of having proper respect for Jan and our family. Now, I have implemented the personal rule of not scheduling anything without checking first with my wife.

Communication with Children

I am very proud of both of my children, Mandy and Rob. They are now out of the teenage stage and have moved on to the early years of adulthood. Both are faithful disciples of Jesus Christ, and I know that God has great plans for their lives. At various times, however, each of them has been spiritually challenged by sin that was serious enough to put their souls in jeopardy.

Although the root sins were quite different, I realized that there was a glaringly common challenge for both children. My wife and I had created high expectations for them. We had regular family devotionals and prayed with them nightly when they were young. We did our best to follow the Scriptures and "train a child in the way he should go" (Proverbs 22:6). We also tried to provide a good personal example for our children to follow and discussed with them our commitment to following God. By all accounts, we were doing a good job and both children became disciples.

However, one topic we never discussed with them was our failures. We were eager to share with them our successes in sharing our faith, but were reluctant to discuss our long bouts of fruitlessness. We urged them to do well in school, but never brought up the time that I nearly dropped out of pharmacy school after being put on academic probation. When we did talk about failures, it was usually theirs that were the focus of conversation. In our family, failure was not really an acceptable option. We were not trying to be overly strict or harsh; we simply wanted to uphold the standard of Jesus Christ in the lives of our children. As a consequence, our children learned to be silent about sinful behaviors that they knew would be unacceptable to us.

When their sins were finally exposed, both children expressed great relief that the truth was finally out, because they had been unable to envision telling us on their own. Once the truth was uncovered, my wife and I were eager to comfort and forgive, and our family was stronger than ever. However, we had to face up to the fact that we had created an unopen atmosphere for our family. We had established unspoken rules of engagement that made some areas of their lives unsafe for discussion. In retrospect, I think that we were more interested in what we wanted our children to be, rather than who they really were. To them, our love must have felt like it had certain performance requirements attached to it.

I am confident that we taught our children properly about the true commitment of a disciple, but we were less careful in teaching them about grace and forgiveness. These factors combined to produce communication barriers in our family that I am just now beginning to understand. Without question, parental responsibility includes setting standards for our children, but we must learn to do so in a way that keeps them close, rather than driving them away through our unrelatability.

I believe open communication becomes increasingly important as our children grow through the teenage years and enter college or the workforce. There is a natural growth process for children that involves gaining independence from their parents. Indeed, in Genesis 2:24, marriage is described as a leaving of father and mother. If we resist this God-ordained separation in the wrong way, I believe we will quickly drive our children away from our values and spiritual beliefs.

As I look back over my life, it is hard to find a time when I grew spiritually more than during my freshman year of college. I experienced an intense period of reevaluation of my own beliefs. I realized that relying on my parents' beliefs was no longer satisfying. I felt compelled to discover a faith of my own. Likewise, I have urged my children to be sure that their faith is genuine and truly theirs—all the while praying that they will not reject the truth of the Bible. These times require open communication and great acceptance on the part of both parent and child. This type of openness is not built overnight, but is cultivated through repeated opportunities of showing your children that your love for them is unconditional.

The Long View

I graduated from law school in 1984 on my birthday. It was a fantastic day! My parents and in-laws had come to town to join in the celebration, and my wife had prepared a glorious reception after the graduation ceremony. I remember the feeling of personal satisfaction that all the hard work had paid off. However, my greatest memory of that day is when I gave Jan an opal ring to thank her for her many acts of support and understanding in helping me to make it through law school. Through the tears of that special moment, I gained a glimpse of God's perspective on the priority that marriage and family should have in the life of a professional. It is a view that sustains me to this day.

John Martin and his wife, Tracy, live in Newton, Massachusetts, with their two children, Rachel, 9, and David, 6. John became a disciple as a teen in North Carolina in 1978. He is a 1985 graduate of North Carolina State University, finishing first in his class at the College of Design. He and Tracy then moved to Boston where he completed a master of architecture degree at Harvard.

In Boston, John has served as a Bible Talk leader, family group leader, house church leader and regional deacon of finance. He currently serves on the Boston church's board of directors. John works with Elkus/ Manfredi Architects.

10 Relationships

Shallow or Soul-Deep?

John Martin

One of the greatest benefits of being a Christian is being able to enjoy relationships that transcend superficiality. As a disciple, it is possible to have many friends who are "closer than a brother" (Proverbs 18:24). Although these relationships are gifts from God, they are not attained without effort.

Throughout the Bible, great men have built great relationships. David and Jonathan, Jesus and John, and Paul and Timothy are all spiritual heroes who enjoyed relationships that surpassed friendships and became "soulships."[1] David had thirty mighty men, but none like Jonathan. Jesus had twelve apostles, but none as close to him as John. And Paul mentored numerous evangelists, but had no one like Timothy. I believe the same principles that allowed these relationships to take their place in history will build great soulships today.

Respect

Many years ago, when I was single and anxious about whom I would marry, a wise man advised me to "concentrate on *being* the right person, not on *finding* the right person." I became a best friend to Tracy whom I later married. But I have never forgotten that advice and have also applied it to building great friendships with brothers in the kingdom, as well as with coworkers.

The first key to building a great relationship is to *be* an admirable man or woman. Paul counseled Titus and Timothy to seek out young men, older men and women "worthy of respect" to befriend. What makes a man or woman "worthy of respect"? He or she is honest, dedicated, humble, disciplined and righteous. Although each of us has our own unique gifts and talents

103

that allow us to excel in some areas, God asks that we do our best in *every* area. For example:

- You may not have an outgoing personality, but you can be cordial to coworkers, neighbors and disciples alike.
- You might not be an intellectual, but you can read the newspaper and be informed about relevant issues and events.
- You might not be able to afford designer suits, but you can be well groomed and dress appropriately. You may not be able to afford the nicest car, apartment or house, but the one you have can be clean and well maintained.
- You may not be a great athlete, but you can watch what you eat, exercise and keep yourself in shape.
- You may not be able to write big checks to charities, but you can take a meal to an elderly person.
- You may not be asked to lead a meeting, but you can be on time for it.

In the week prior to writing this chapter, I was convicted about the issue of punctuality. David Manfredi (the owner of the architectural firm that I work for) and I were discussing when to take a cab for a client meeting. The meeting was scheduled for 9:00 AM, but our client joked that we would be foolish to actually show up at that time because the meeting was certain to start late. On the day of the meeting, David suggested we call a cab at 8:30, giving us plenty of time to arrive by 9:00. I argued for a later departure, hoping to get some last minute work done. I reminded him that the client had suggested that we be late. He asked me, "John, if your client suggested you smoke a cigarette, would you do it?" "Of course not!" I replied, gagging. "Why not?" he continued. "Because it's unhealthy, addictive and offensive," I responded. "So is being late," he said.

Look at the first two chapters of Titus. Paul uses the words "self-controlled" five times in these short chapters. He also uses other words like "hospitable, holy, disciplined, temperate, pure, kind, trusted, upright, and godly." Do these adjectives describe a man or woman you would like to know? Personal integrity characterized the lives of David, Paul and Jesus. Disciples or not, we are drawn to men like these. We admire them. We want to be like them. And if these qualities characterize our lives, people will be drawn to us as well. A life worthy of respect and imitation is the first key to building a great relationship.

Care

A second key to great relationships is care. People need to feel and to know that you care and that you care for them specifically. The men who have most affected my life have been those who cared for me the most. My father, my eleventh-grade math teacher, the two men who studied the Bible with me, my best friend in college, and various ministers, evangelists and disciples along the way—all demonstrated a personal interest in my life. Their expressed love shaped me and created emotional bonds with me that I cherish to this day.

Jeff Chappell is one of these men. I first met Jeff in January 1991, when he came into our ministry as an intern. His genuine warmth and concern for everyone around him quickly won my heart. He constantly poured his heart out to serve my family. When our first child, Rachel, was born in June 1992, he was the first to visit in the hospital. Jeff and I did everything together, from playing pickup football to many late-night talks. All along, he continued to serve. When I was in over my head in a kitchen renovation project, Jeff was there to hang doors and frame windows. When our second child, David, was born, Jeff and his family took care of every little detail, making sure that all the loose ends were picked up. He taught me woodworking, and his basement woodshop became the birthplace of a special piece of furniture that became my anniversary present one year for Tracy.

When I became a regional deacon in 1997, Jeff presented me with an inscribed Bible. He had discipled me with great love and patience. When I was certain that I was right and Tracy was wrong in parenting situations, Jeff was the one who had the long talks with me, showed me that I was the one in the wrong, and got me back on track. When my mom died in 1999, Jeff helped me make sense of it all.

During the ten years that I have known Jeff, I have seen him raise two devout children and be raised up to be an evangelist in the Boston church. I have been with him in good times and bad. We have baptized people together. We have gone on family vacations together. We have wondered where God was taking us and then been "wondered" by the results. During these ten years, Jeff has been in my ministry and in probably six or seven others. He has lived in three houses and three different towns, yet he has never stopped discipling me. Jeff now lives in another city, but our hearts are forever linked by love and the time that God gave us together. Jeff's love reminds me of Paul's love for the Thessalonians:

> ...but we were gentle among you, like a mother caring for her little children. We loved you so much that we were delighted to share with you not only the gospel of God but our lives as well, because you had become so dear to us. Surely you remember, brothers, our toil and hardship; we worked night and day in order not to be a burden to anyone while we preached the gospel of God to you.
>
> You are witnesses, and so is God, of how holy, righteous and blameless we were among you who believed. For you know that we dealt with each of you as a father deals with his own children, encouraging, comforting and urging you to live lives worthy of God, who calls you into his kingdom and glory. (1 Thessalonians 2:7–12)

Would you have liked to have been a part of this church? Paul's love was evident. He encouraged. He comforted. And he urged people to follow God. This is how he built great relationships.

Whenever I seek to build a new relationship, I think about Paul's work with the Thessalonians and the example Jeff set for me, asking myself the following questions:

- Do I consider the other person better than I?
- Do I think about the other's goals, concerns, desires and feelings?

- Am I willing to sacrifice my time, my money and my agenda to truly serve and love and meet another's needs?
- Am I consistent and patient in reaching out to them again and again, even when my initiative is not rewarded by a response?
- Do I love unconditionally?
- Does the other feel my love, or do my intentions remain within me, unexpressed?

These principles all apply to everyone at work. Very few managers in the world take the time to get to know their employees as individuals. Last year, I made a decision that I would remember all my staff's birthdays. I asked my assistant to make a list of all the birthdays on our team, and I put them into my calendar. Now, on each person's birthday, I take ten minutes to write down specifically what I think that person has brought to our team that year and leave the card for him to discover on his desk as he arrives that morning. What began as a small gesture has turned out to have a big effect. I have taken great satisfaction in seeing the pleasantly shocked reactions.

I am confident that I can build a great relationship with anyone if I will pour myself out for him or her, as Jeff did for me and as Paul did for the Thessalonians. They will then understand the depth of my love and be open to the final aspect of great friendships: growth.

Growth

A relationship characterized by mutual respect and care for one another will be rewarding. It will not, however, have reached its full potential with just these two ingredients. Great relationships add growth as a third ingredient. A great relationship is synergistic, with both parties growing from their interaction. The men and women who have changed my life the most have challenged me, but always in a context of respect and love. I have listened to difficult evaluations of my pride, deceit, lack of love, selfishness and cowardice, but the comments that have made the difference have all come with gentleness, not demands. David obviously taught Jonathan, Jesus taught John (and everyone else), and Paul taught Timothy. Yet, without doubt, David drew strength from Jonathan, Jesus drew strength from John, and Paul drew strength from Timothy.

A great friend knows what you need. David was a mighty warrior, yet when he was exhausted, dejected and hiding at Horesh while being hunted by a mad king, 1 Samuel 23:16 simply and beautifully says, "Jonathan went to David at Horesh and helped him find strength in God." What do you think Jonathan might have said to David? Somehow, Jonathan was able to comfort and inspire him. He was able to get David to a spiritual level that David alone was unable to attain.

Ken Lowey is a successful chiropractor in the Boston area and a great friend. Back in the early 1990s, Michael Firkins (another architect) and I designed a clinic for his practice. Ken and I became close during the process, and I have always valued our friendship. I admire his accomplishments, both within the church and in the community. And during a lunch in July 2000, Ken changed my life.

Being a successful architect has always been a driving force in my life. I knew I wanted to be an architect when I was four years old. One of the most cutting questions that the brothers had asked me when I was studying the Bible as a teenager was, "What if becoming a Christian meant giving up architecture?" That was without a doubt the most difficult cost I counted. I was willing to give it up, however. I made a decision at that point that architecture would never come between me and my God, that the kingdom would always come first.

God has subsequently blessed that teenage, small–town decision by bringing me much further beyond my dreams than I could have imagined. So much beyond my dreams that in the summer of 2000, some real opportunities had begun to open up. My buildings were being built, I had good relationships with clients, and I had for the first time reached financial security. Many were asking me when I would go out and start my own firm. The door was open and I was ready to walk through it. I prayed about it. I talked to many disciples about it. Tracy, however, had some reservations. We talked at length about all the plusses and minuses. I told her that I wanted to be like Ken Lowey—with a successful practice, professional honors and recognition from his peers, the dictating of his own hours, and the serving of the church with a flexibility that I did not enjoy as long as I "worked for someone else." She encouraged me to have lunch with him and bounce my ideas off him. I thought that this was a great idea, and frankly, I thought he would encourage me to be bold and go for it.

Nope. Ken "helped me find strength in God." He told me about how hard the formative years of his practice were: the long hours and the painful headaches. He started his office when he was unmarried, without children, and not yet a disciple. It owned him; he did not own it. He also went on to tell me how his teenage children (who are disciples) are now, in good ways, growing away from him. He takes every opportunity he can to drive them to their various events and practices, just to get time with them because their schedules are packed with school and kingdom commitments. "John, your children are four and eight. Don't miss your opportunity to be with them as much as you can during these vital years."

There was more. He said he knew me, how driven I was and how many sacrifices I had made for the kingdom. "But I have noticed, John, that you always figure out a way to accomplish what is best for you. You put the kingdom before your career, but I'm not sure you always put your family before it. You tend to make your decisions based upon what is best for the kingdom and for yourself. You should train yourself to think about what is best for the kingdom and your family instead." I was stunned. Everything now came into focus!

Initially, I could not understand why Tracy was reluctant to encourage or even acquiesce to my professional dreams. After all, wouldn't more money, more professional recognition and more political power be good for us? Well, not if it came at the expense of being fully engaged with her and the children. Not if it meant long hours, flying back and forth across the country on business trips, and always flying back and forth between the house and the office in my mind! I was both disappointed and excited. My dream would once again have to take a back seat. But the excitement was palpable as I realized all the pain that one lunch saved me. I do not know whether my dream to direct my own firm is dead or just deferred, but I promised Ken (and God) that day that I would not "leave my children." After they leave us, Tracy and I will reevaluate, but I will always put my family before my profession. I will always ask, "What is best for my family?" rather than "What is best for my career?"

I grew a lot that day. I trust Ken and I know that he loves me. Yet the growth came because he loved me so much that he was not afraid to challenge me.

Soulships

Respect, care and growth: these three keys can unlock many seemingly impenetrable doors. I am consistently amazed by others' responses to these principles. People who initially seem cold, distant or preoccupied suddenly warm up when they feel that they can respect and trust you, that you care for them, and that your influence can make a positive difference in their lives. God promises great friendships if we will live our lives in a manner worthy of respect, pour out our hearts in words and acts of service, and then gently instruct, encourage and admonish one another. While working hard to enrich other's lives, our own joy will be abundant.

Note

[1] I owe the term "soulship" to Michael Voligny, a close friend with whom I share such a relationship. He coined the term in a paper he wrote for a class at Harvard University.

John Beggs received his BS in engineering physics from Cornell University in 1985. He taught high school-level science and math in Western Samoa while in the Peace Corps, 1986–1988. John then received his PhD in behavioral neuroscience from Yale University in 1998. He currently works as a postdoctoral fellow in a laboratory at the National Institute of Health in Bethesda, Maryland, studying Parkinson's disease. John has been married to his wife, Sara, since 1996 and has been a Christian since 1990, having become in a disciple in New York.

Thomas Darling is assistant professor of dermatology at the Uniformed Services University of the Health Sciences in Bethesda, Maryland. He received his MD and PhD from Duke University in 1990. Following an internship in medicine at University of North Carolina Hospitals and a dermatology residency at Duke, he completed a research fellowship within the Dermatology Branch, National Cancer Institute, National Institutes of Health. At USUHS since 1999, Tom directs the Sulzberger Laboratory for Dermatologic Research, studying the molecular basis of skin tumors and familial tumor syndromes. He is a dermatology consultant at NIH, USUHS, National Naval Medical Center and Walter Reed Army Medical Center, where he teaches dermatology to medical students and residents.

Tom's wife, Miki, is also a physician. They have two children, Paul and Alexis. Thomas became a disciple in 1988 in Durham, North Carolina.

11 Evangelism

In a Professional Setting

John Beggs and Thomas Darling

Lipsett Amphitheater at the National Institutes of Health (NIH) in Bethesda, Maryland, is where thousands of top-flight scientists and Nobel laureates have presented groundbreaking scientific discoveries. But this was the first time for this location to host a teacher who just as persuasively expounded earthshaking Biblical truths. Douglas Jacoby gave a talk entitled "Textual, Historical and Scientific Evidence for the Bible" to a crowd of critical scientists. We were thrilled to be a part of this event, and God had worked mightily to get our coworkers there.

The Challenge

As disciples, we all want our coworkers to come to know Jesus, but sharing our faith in a professional atmosphere can test that very faith. People are busy, focused on tasks and deadlines. They don't appear interested in deeper issues. It can be frightening to ask your boss what he or she thinks about God. They may think, "How dare he, as my underling, try to tell me what to do with my life?" Will they ridicule us? Deny us promotion? Will the office ostracize us? Yet, we are confident that God has entrusted us with answers for their lives and has given us the strength and confidence to share these answers with them.

As scientists, we have struggled with these issues and how to be most effective in reaching out to others in the workplace. Scientists tend to be irreligious. In a 1996 survey, less than ten percent of scientists said that they believed in a God who answered prayers and in personal immortality! From our personal experience, we have found that most scientists view religious people as uneducated, ignorant and superstitious cultural anachronisms. Perhaps you can relate to this at your workplace.

Be All Things to All Men

How would you evangelize in such an environment? Pray really hard and hope that someone notices you? Print up hundreds of pamphlets and blitz the workplace? Mention Jesus casually in every sentence? We tried these strategies without much success. What we have found most effective is modeled after Paul's admonition in 1 Corinthians 9:22: "I have become all things to all men so that by all possible means I might save some."

As a practical matter, this means thinking about and acting on the needs of people in your workplace. For example, scientists like information and logical arguments. To meet this need, we hosted a series of lectures on issues like: The Problem of Pain, Evolution and the Bible, Philosophy and Philosophers, The Reliability of the Bible. Each lecture was delivered very professionally with a PowerPoint presentation. Refreshments were served beforehand and a question and answer session followed. Announcements were posted and published in calendars of upcoming events. At the end of each session a sign-up sheet was circulated so that we could create an e-mail list to inform attendees of future talks and events. We also hosted more "fun" events where we could develop closer friendships.

Many people we work with will not come to any church–sponsored event, and yet the time we spend with them can still be influential. At NIH, many topics with spiritual dimensions are often discussed such as sexual orientation, stem cell research, evolution and mental illness. Reading about these topics in advance can help us to bring a Biblical perspective to the discussion. These topics might not be burning issues in your workplace and they may not touch your coworkers at the heart level. In that case, consider *their* needs—it might be more relevant to discuss lessons you have learned regarding marriage, raising kids or how to handle anger and forgiveness in work relationships. Having deep, personal discussions from a spiritual perspective may form the groundwork for them to start examining their own relationship with God. These discussions can often be more influential in the long run than merely repeating a previously rejected invitation to church.

Although we are quite familiar with rejection, God has blessed these efforts to transform the ministry at NIH. During the past three years, God has increased the NIH ministry from one disciple to several, including five PhDs, a veterinarian, a computer specialist and a research scientist.

Be a Fool for Christ

While it is an act of love to be all things to all people, God's truth is inherently countercultural in a fallen world. As stated by Paul, the message of the cross is foolishness to the world (1 Corinthians 1:23) and we are "fools for Christ" (1 Corinthians 4:10). No matter how incisive our arguments or persuasive our speaking, our message will still be rejected by many. We need to remember that we did not become disciples to gain the respect and approval of others, but the approval of God. Indeed, we are destined to "get grief" for sharing our faith in the workplace, as the following incidents illustrate.

It was late on a Friday and people were starting to head home, so I [John] thought I could slip into my boss' office for a quick discussion before he left. He was an accomplished man, a leading expert on the brain and a professor at an Ivy League school. I naively thought that he would enjoy being asked for his opinions about God. "About who?!" he bitterly shot back. "I don't ever want to hear you use that word again when you are in this lab. I've heard that you are inviting people to your discussion groups, and I want you to stop. If there was a little switch in the back of your head that could turn you off of religion, I would flip it in an instant!" He continued his diatribe for about half an hour, and I left his office in a daze, scared that he would try to throw me out of graduate school.

During the years that followed, I continued to discuss God with other people in his lab, sometimes even in his presence. He mellowed and eventually expressed regret about how he reacted in our first encounter. By the time I left his lab, we had had several lengthy discussions about God, and he had started to attend a nearby church. Although he is not a disciple, he has opened up dramatically and we are friends. During that time, I also was able to study the Bible with several lab members.

In my next laboratory position, I thought I could invite the lab chief to our Christmas service since he had sounded interested when asked I him to church a few weeks before. I was a little scared as I clutched the small invitation, so I prayed before I entered his office. His reaction was anything but mild. "You make me very uncomfortable," he said as he folded his arms and pushed back quickly in his rolling chair. "You know you are not allowed to bring up matters of religion in a government work-place," he snapped. "You can't go around telling people that your way is the only way—you have to stop this at once." Thrown off guard, I nervously asked, "Is there a law against me inviting peo-ple to church?" "Well, no," he mumbled. "Then I will obey God rather than you," I answered, almost disbelieving the words that came out of my mouth. I continued, "I know that there is a God and that people need him in their lives, so I will keep talking about him. I do not mean to be insubordinate, but I must do what is right." I left his office shaking and worried that he would try to damage my career. My worries actually caused me to pray more, and during the next few months I continued to invite fellow lab mates. We eventually started a lunchtime Bible talk that met at a picnic table outside. He has walked past our table several times— but has said nothing.

While being a fool for Christ means not being ashamed of the gospel, it also means obedience and trust in the face of rejection. After a harsh encounter with one coworker, it is very tempting to stop sharing with others. Of course we must be sensitive to not come across as too religious, but God commands us to be fishers of men. Practical ways in which you can show that you are not ashamed of the gospel would include leaving your Bible on your desk to prompt conversations, mentioning that you attend church, or attending any spiritual events at work like the recent national day of prayer or previously established Bible discussion groups. It is also better to mention that you are a Christian soon after beginning a new job rather than waiting too long—Jesus was very direct about who he was, and we should be too.

Zeal

Many of us want to be more effective in our evangelism at the workplace. We know others who seem to always have good news to share about someone who is open to the gospel or who was just baptized. We may wonder, "Why aren't greater things happening at my workplace? Am I doing all that I can?" Of course, past performance is no guarantee of future success, and results may vary. But we can gauge our hearts.

For example, imagine the person who, to your knowledge, is the most zealous for Christ. Leave out your evangelist or elder for the moment, and think of someone in a secular position, perhaps a recent convert. (Don't read on until you have a name and a face in your mind.) Now imagine that person showing up at your workplace. He or she gets a job just down the hall from you. Most of us would be filled with joy to share the workplace with a zealous disciple. But how would you feel? Would you be embarrassed by the number of people that didn't even know you were a Christian? Or would you be ashamed to be associated with the new guy who keeps talking about Jesus? If either of these thoughts come to you, there is work to be done. You may not have the opportunity to have that person join your work, but you could invite him or her to visit you at work. Just having that person show up will change how you feel about work and challenge you in your evangelism. Perhaps you could share your faith together or even start a Bible study at work.

God Reliance

Reaching out to others is always a balance between becoming like them (so that they will be more willing to listen) and yet retaining a Christlike character (so that they will be drawn to something greater). We can be confident that God will help us in our task.

> For God did not give us a spirit of timidity, but a spirit of power, of love and of self-discipline. (2 Timothy 1:7)

Cecil A. Wooten began working for Chicago Bridge & Iron Company (CBI) while still in high school. After distinguished service in World War II, he completed a degree in engineering at the University of Alabama. Continuing his work with CBI, by 1962 he had become managing director of CBI's British subsidiary in London. After returning to the US, he was appointed manager of the Houston sales district and was given a place on CBI's board of directors, which he continued to hold until his retirement in 1983. He eventually served as senior vice president, overseeing such issues as commercial development and corporate administration.

Cecil became a disciple in 1978, and after retirement from CBI, he became director of development for Christian Family Services in Gainesville, Florida. After helping plant a new church in Denver, he his wife, Helen, moved to Boston in 1988 where Cecil became administrator for the Boston Church of Christ. A year later he helped to establish worldwide administrative policies for the fast-growing International Churches of Christ. From 1994 to 2000, he served as leader of the world sector administrators for this family of churches.

Cecil and Helen have five children: Michael, Margaret, Martin, Marsha and Mark—and twelve grandchildren.

12 Courage

Do the Right Thing

Cecil A. Wooten

My career in the business world began in September 1941, when at age seventeen, I was employed by Chicago Bridge & Iron Company (CBI) in Birmingham, Alabama, working twenty hours per week after school as a file clerk in the drafting department. By the end of my senior year, I was promoted from file clerk to junior draftsman, as I had learned to produce simple designs and drawings. After I graduated from high school in May 1942, I went to work for CBI full-time. But in the fall of 1942 with the whole world at war, I received notice to report to the army. My work with CBI had to be put on hold.

Time to Sink or Swim

After being wounded in November 1944, in Germany, and returning to combat December 1944, just in time for the Battle of the Bulge, I was wounded again in January 1945. In April 1945, I was commissioned second lieutenant. Infantry. When the war ended in Europe, I remained in Germany for another year and was promoted to first lieutenant. I eventually returned in September 1946 to work at CBI as a full-time draftsman. I also entered engineering school at the University of Alabama on a full-time basis under the GI Bill. Thirty months later I graduated with a bachelor's degree in mechanical engineering. At that time I had eight and a half years of service credit with CBI. While I was a student, Helen and I were married.

Upon graduation, I was transferred to the CBI New York office where I was assigned to the Export Department as a contracting engineer (salesman) to be trained for export sales to the Caribbean area and Central and South America. After about a year of estimating and proposal writing, my office manager, a

vice president and director of CBI, handed me an inquiry request-
ing a proposal for the supply, fabrication and on-site construction of a number of crude-oil and refined-product steel storage
tanks required for a new grassroots refinery to be built in Puerto
Rico. I was instructed to estimate the cost, determine the selling
price, provide a promised completion date, prepare the quota-
tion, sign the proposal and to represent CBI to the customer in
any negotiations.

I was twenty-seven years old, one year out of engineering
school, the youngest employee in the office by ten or more years,
with one year of training as a contracting engineer—and for the
first time completely responsible for a major proposal. After
finishing the estimates and drafting the proposal, I asked my office
manager to review my work before I submitted the proposal to the
customer. My quote was $2.3 million, which was equivalent to
more than seven percent of the New York office's total annual
sales volume. My office manager took my draft proposal from me,
put it on his desk and asked me if I felt confident with my estimate
and proposal. I told him that I had done my best. He picked up the
proposal without having opened it and instructed me to submit it
and wished me luck. It was time for me to sink or swim.

About two weeks after the proposal was submitted, I arranged
to have lunch with the customer's purchasing manager. On my
arrival at a midtown Manhattan restaurant, I discovered that the
purchasing manager had brought two friends with him. His
friends were salesmen who had submitted proposals for other
components of the Puerto Rican refinery. They were not competing for the tankage. It was evident that the three of them had con-
sumed several drinks before I had arrived. I ordered a tomato
juice because I was (and still am) a nondrinker. They ordered
more alcoholic drinks and became increasingly boisterous.

After about an hour, they were still drinking and had not
ordered any food. The purchasing manager revealed to me that
his two drinking companions were each to be awarded contracts
to supply pipe and valves for the new refinery. He questioned if I
was really interested in supplying the tankage. I told him I was.

He spoke very loudly and could be heard by everyone in the room. He said that he might be able to negotiate a contract with CBI for the tankage if I would have two drinks with him. The room became silent, with everyone looking at us. After a few seconds, I rose from the table and replied, "I had expected CBI to receive the award on the basis of a competitive price, a reputation for on-time completion, high quality engineering and workmanship. If the award requires that I consume two drinks, then I must pass." I excused myself and left without paying the bill for the drinks.

I took the subway to my downtown office and went directly to report to my office manager. I was very nervous, thinking that my job could be in jeopardy. After I finished my report, my manager stated, "That man is a fool. Your response was in order."

The next morning, shortly after my arrival at the office, the phone rang. It was the customer's purchasing manager. Without any mention of the previous day's incident, he said he was awarding CBI the contract for the tankage at our quoted price and gave me a purchase order number. One year later, before CBI had completed the tankage contract, the Puerto Rican refinery was doubled in size. The customer's purchasing manager negotiated with me, without competition, all of the additional tankage required. During the next several years, the purchasing manager and I developed a close working relationship based on friendship and trust. I believe the lesson here is that you can always have more impact on people when you have courage to do what is right.

Let Your 'Yes' Be Yes, Your 'No,' No

In late 1956, our family (which would soon include five children) moved to London and I was named managing director of CBI's British subsidiary responsible for Europe, Africa, the Middle East and Southeast Asia. I was thirty-two years old. Except for my experience in World War II as a combat infantry platoon leader, I had no previous management or corporate financial training. I was not familiar with balance sheets, cash flow, payroll systems or personnel policies. Again, I was in over my head and again, it was sink or swim time.

In mid-December 1959, I received a telephone call from the managing director of a London-based subsidiary of a US engineering company. He asked me to meet him and several other staff at his London office the next morning. At 9:00 AM the next day, I was informed that the customer, an engineering firm, had been asked by a London-based oil refinery owner to submit a bid covering the design, engineering, procurement and management of construction of a new grassroots oil refinery in the Rhur Valley in Germany. Two German engineering companies were submitting competitive bids directly to the refinery owner. It was thought that the German engineering competitors were receiving favorable treatment from the German tank builders who had quoted lower tank prices to the German engineering firm than they were quoting to our London customer. Also, the three German tank builders had divided the tankage proposal among themselves with each quoting only one-third of the tankage to our London customer.

I was asked about CBI's experience with constructing tanks in Germany. Our experience was limited to purchasing German steel and tank fabrication for export with the tankage to be constructed at oil facilities outside of Germany. CBI had performed no erection of tankage in Germany because the German oil companies had favored the German tank builders and CBI had not been given the opportunity to bid.

CBI was asked to submit a bid for the procurement, supply and construction of the German refinery tankage as a check of the prices our customer had received from the German tank builders. CBI's bid was required within seven days to allow our customer to meet the due date for submitting their proposal to the refinery owner. After my review of the specifications and proposal request, I agreed to submit a bid with some rather far-reaching stipulations, the most important of which was that one hundred percent of the tankage would be awarded to us if the refinery contract was awarded to our customer.

After an attempt was made to persuade me to submit a bid without these conditions, an understanding was reached. If CBI prices and delivery were used in the successful bid for the refinery, CBI would be awarded one hundred percent of the tankage. The following Friday, the seventh day, the CBI verbal price ($12 million) and completion promise (eighteen months after receipt of order) was submitted.

Four days later, I was asked to meet with our customer to discuss the CBI verbal proposal. Since CBI had no previous construction experience in Germany, the customer was concerned about CBI's ability to deal with German labor, laws and regulations, safety standards, design and quality control requirements. Because of this concern, I was asked if CBI would accept a penalty clause in the tankage contract stipulating that for each week the construction went beyond the promised completion date, the contract price would be reduced by $100,000. I agreed to accept the penalty clause, provided that the customer would accept a bonus clause that would increase the contract price by $100,000 each week the construction was completed before the promised completion date. With the addition of the bonus and penalty clauses, our customer agreed to name CBI as the tank supplier and constructor for all of the tankage and would award the contract to CBI for $12 million if our customer was the successful bidder. A few days later, CBI submitted a formal written proposal confirming our understanding, price and completion date.

In January 1960, a month later, I was called to our customer's office to meet with the purchasing manager. I was informed that our customer had been awarded the contract to build the German refinery. In awarding the refinery contract to our customer, the refinery owner had required that at least fifty percent of the tankage be awarded to the German tank builders. The purchasing manager indicated that his hands were tied, but he had prepared a purchase order for CBI in the amount of $6 million, covering fifty percent of the tankage. This price was twice the amount of any previous single contract executed by CBI's British subsidiary. What a dilemma! Should I accept the order for only half the tankage?

I reminded the purchasing manager that he had attended all of the previous meetings held with his managing director and had received CBI's written proposal outlining the agreement reached. I stated, "CBI was to be awarded one hundred percent of the tankage—not fifty percent. CBI had kept its word and expected you to keep yours. If you accepted the refinery contract knowing you had an agreement with CBI, it appears you have breached our agreement. Since you used our competitive price and delivery, CBI was instrumental in your being the successful bidder. If you had not had CBI's price, you would have been forced to use the higher prices and longer deliveries submitted by the German tank builders. You also would have three German tank builders on the construction site as opposed to one if CBI were to do the tankage." I then stated, "CBI could not accept the award of anything less than one hundred percent of the tankage for the price of $12 million, which was the basis of our agreement. If you wish to discuss this matter further, please phone me. I will be at my office."

Several days later, the managing director asked me to come to his office to discuss the tankage contract. I was advised that upon my refusal to accept an order for half of the tankage, our customer realized that the German tank builders combined had insufficient capacity to complete the tankage on time—it would take them six to twelve months longer than CBI's promised completion time of eighteen months. With this information, the refinery owner approved CBI's award of one hundred percent of the tankage. Our customer's managing director apologized for compromising our prebid agreement. He also said that CBI's very competitive tankage price and speedy construction time had been a crucial factor in their successful negotiation. CBI completed the construction three weeks early, which (with the bonus clause) raised the final contract price to $12.3 million. During the next three years, CBI was a successful bidder for all of the tankage required for three additional grassroots German refineries for other refinery owners. It often requires courage to do the right thing, but the long term impact can be significant.

Courage to Repent
From my initial position as a part-time file clerk in the drafting department to my final position as senior vice president of

administration and member of the board of directors, my forty-three-year career at CBI provided many opportunities to test my courage in the business setting. However, one of my biggest challenges lay outside the realm of business. I had learned to have courage in the corporate setting, but would I have the same courage when it came to my relationship with my family and my relationship with God? During my climb up the corporate ladder, I had failed miserably as a husband and father, as most of my focus had been devoted to my corporation, with my family receiving only what was left over. Because of my extensive travel schedule, I became an absentee father and husband—sometimes gone for weeks at a time to some location halfway around the world.

Though I considered myself religious and a Christian, I left my family to fend for themselves, as I provided no moral or spiritual leadership. In the late 1960s and early 1970s, my family had disintegrated to the point that I had no relationship with any of my children. As soon as they reached eighteen, they each left home and were basically on their own. All of my children were involved with drugs in one way or another. One was arrested for armed robbery and a daughter became pregnant in high school. At one point, Helen told me she had tired of trying to be mother and father to the children and since it appeared as if I felt no responsibility for leading the family, she wanted a divorce.

In the early 1970s, I came to the realization that if I was going to salvage my marriage and my relationship with my children, it was necessary for me to make a radical change in my life focus. I sought help and input from the church leaders of my denomination where I served as an elder. Sadly, this source of help turned out to be no help at all.

About that time our middle son had been baptized into Christ and was enrolled in Oklahoma Christian College. He encouraged me to open the Bible and helped me to search for answers. Four years later, in 1978, my wife and I were both baptized into Christ in Chicago and became a part of the new Chicago Church of Christ when it was planted in 1982. At age fifty-four, I began a new life. I am happy to say that as we studied the Bible, my wife and I were reconciled, and as of April 4, 2002, we will have been married for fifty-five years. It took a number of years after we became disciples for me to seek and receive the forgiveness of each of my five children. But this has resulted in the establishment of very close, personal relationships with each of them. We have twelve grandchildren. Four of them are baptized disciples. We are hopeful that more will be baptized into Christ in the next few years.

The courage to face my own shortcomings as the spiritual leader of my family led me to one of the most rewarding periods of my professional life. When I retired from CBI, I also retired from the board of trustees of a university, board of directors of an Illinois bank, board of directors of a worldwide deep-sea diving and undersea repair company, as well as from several nonprofit organizations. In April 1983, two weeks after retirement, my wife and I moved to Gainesville, Florida. I became director of development for Christian Family Services, an adoption agency affiliated with the Crossroads Church of Christ.

Then in 1986, Helen and I moved from Gainesville, Florida, to Denver, Colorado, to help plant a new congregation, the Denver Church of Christ. At the request of the elders of the Boston Church of Christ, Helen and I then moved to Boston, Massachusetts, in 1988. I became office manager and administrator of the Boston church. In 1989, I was asked to help establish worldwide administration policy for the International Churches of Christ. I was named leader of the world sector administrators, a position I held until the year 2000, when I felt it necessary to reduce my administrative responsibilities after Helen suffered a severe stroke.

As I consider the role courage has played during the course of my life, I can see that God has been faithful to me every time I have had the courage to be faithful to him. My encouragement to you is the same as the apostle Paul wrote in I Corinthians 16:13–14, "Be on your guard; stand firm in the faith; be men of courage; be strong. Do everything in love."

Shelley Metten has been married thirty-one years to her husband, Greg, a veterinarian. They have two children: Jennifer, 26, who is married to Benoni Pantoja and they have a baby boy, Micah; and Matthew, 25, who is married to Brooke.

Shelley became a Christian in 1980 in San Diego, California, along with Greg. In 1985, their family moved to the Boston church in order to train to be missionaries in India. They served as missionaries in India for five years and in Tokyo, Japan, for three years.

Shelley has a master's degree in physiology and a PhD in anatomy. She has served on the faculty at San Diego State University, Harvard Medical School, Tokai Medical School (Tokyo, Japan) and UCLA Medical School, where she is currently an associate professor of medicine.

13 Women Professionals

Journeying to Amazing Places

Shelley Metten

We are all on a path of purification in our walk with God, and I am always intrigued by the course each path takes. Certainly for me, as a woman professional, there have been some interesting turns.

God's Professional Path

I entered college and then professional life at a time when it was not easy for a woman to establish herself and be respected for her abilities. I know for me, it has been many years of tremendous personal sacrifice and diligence to achieve my professional goals. I was raised in a family where, going back many generations, no family member had ever gone to college. In fact, my father believed that women should not go to college and discouraged me in every way.

I had no confidence in my abilities, but knew in my heart that I wanted to accomplish something. I found a way to support myself and go to college with a dream of being a middle–school teacher. At the completion of my first quarter, I had received all As and was invited into the Freshman Honor Society, but I did not know that it was an honor society. I saw the Greek letters on the envelope, thought it was from a sorority and threw out the envelope without opening it. Later that same quarter my zoology professor recognized a science aptitude in me and encouraged me to select biology as my major.

I had taken only one biology course in high school and no chemistry, physics or higher math; but I embarked on this new challenge with lots of determination. I did graduate with a biology degree, but during my senior year, while taking a physiology course, the professor liked my work and encouraged me to do a master's degree in physiology. My husband, Greg, was about to enter veterinary school, and I knew that we would be there for a while, so I agreed to do the master's degree in physiology.

Near the completion of that degree, we gave birth to our daughter, Jennifer. I had received a fellowship for the master's degree and part of my responsibility was teaching a course in the first year veterinary curriculum that included anatomy. The chair of that course liked my work and encouraged me to do a PhD in anatomy. I agreed. A year into my PhD program, we were surprised to find out that we were expecting a second child.

Our son, Matthew, was born just as Greg was completing his veterinary degree, I was completing my PhD and Jennifer was only fourteen months old. I remember middle-of-the-night feedings with my newborn, Matt, in my arms, reciting the Kreb's Cycle (a biochemistry pathway) like it was a nursery rhyme. I would take one baby to the university and do my research all night while Greg would be home with the other baby. Then I would come home, sleep for a few hours and be with the babies while Greg went to the veterinary hospital to take care of his patients. Those were challenging days, but we completed our degrees and at that time, I was twenty-seven years old.

A Teaching Career Begins

We moved to San Diego, California, because Greg had selected a veterinary practice to join, and typical of me, I had no real plan. I needed to complete some writing on my dissertation, and with two children less than two years old at my feet, very little was getting done. I called San Diego State University to see if I could have some office space in exchange for teaching anatomy. I was immediately hired and quickly promoted. Greg, unfortunately, had become more and more disillusioned with his life, and we began to drift apart. There was a lot of pressure on me because of our marriage problems, my juggling of my schedule with two very young children and my rapidly advancing career. Just at the breaking point...we were invited to church.

Greg and I had many things to work through during the six months that it took for us to become Christians, but on June 29, 1980, everything changed. Even though we were very educated people, our wisdom had nearly cost us our marriage and family. Solomon was right:

> For with much wisdom comes much sorrow;
> the more knowledge, the more grief. (Ecclesiastes 1:18)

When we became disciples, it was clear to us that we had jumped onto a new path. Little did I know that there were going to be some forks in the road that would have to do with my career, the only part of my life that I thought was going well!

God-Directed Moves

Just before I achieved full professor status in San Diego, we were asked to move to Boston, Massachusetts, to train for one of the first mission teams being sent out from the Boston church. Greg was thrilled—I was in shock. A fierce struggle ensued in my heart. I had sacrificed so much during those ten years of college and the fight for my position on a very male-dominated faculty. I wrestled so hard with this decision because I knew that leaving the university under these circumstances would probably mean that I would never be welcomed back onto a faculty again. It made no sense to me to go, but somehow I knew that this call was from God. It was a huge step of faith for me, but that decision was the most important spiritual choice I have ever made. It also turned into the most unbelievable professional opportunity of my career.

When we arrived in Boston, someone suggested that I ask Harvard Medical School if they needed an anatomist for the year. I thought it was a hysterical idea, and just to show how ridiculous it was, I called Harvard. And they hired me! For one year I had the opportunity to teach at the utopia of medical schools with a leading specialist. I was not sure what God was doing, but I could only imagine how much he enjoyed my reaction! I thought I had given up so much, and yet that one year at Harvard Medical School changed my entire future. It was painful to leave when the year was over, but we were on our way to India.

We lived to India for five years, New York for two years, and finally we were back in California (Los Angeles) by the autumn of 1993. The timing seemed right for me to go back to teaching, so I went to UCLA Medical School to see if they would accept me after so many years away from my professional life. They were a little reluctant, but with the Harvard experience on my resume, they hired me. Within four years, I was promoted to associate professor. Two days after my promotion, we were asked to move to Tokyo, Japan—I could not believe it! Our two kids were just getting ready to graduate from UCLA, life seemed settled, and then this. It took a year for me to make a decision. Not only was this becoming a pattern, I was getting older, so it would be more difficult for me to ever return. But I left UCLA and off we went to Tokyo where Greg served as an elder for the Pacific Rim World Sector of the International Churches of Christ.

Solomon Was Right

Three years later we returned to Los Angeles, and once again I humbly went back to UCLA Medical School. My resume now looked like a slice of Swiss cheese, with holes so large between my various university positions that you could question my emotional stability. To my amazement, they welcomed me with open arms and went to great lengths to restore me to my original position. I am once again an associate professor at UCLA Medical School, but it is different now. The position and expectations have not changed, but I am different. It has taken twenty-two years, six moves to cities in three different countries and four university positions for me to begin to understand what it means to trust God's wisdom rather than my own. Solomon's conclusion was right:

> Now all has been heard;
> here is the conclusion of the matter:
> Fear God and keep his commandments,
> for this is the whole duty of man. (Ecclesiastes 12:13)

It is probably no surprise that today my marriage is wonder-ful. My children are married to disciples, and all of them are in the ministry. We are in the AMS (Arts, Media and Sports) region in Los Angeles where Greg is a regional elder and we lead the family supersector (I'll let you guess what that means). We love the people and we love our life.

I do not know where you are in your professional life, but I do know this: Accept the path that God has planned for you. When the confusing forks in the road appear, fear God and keep his commandments. His wisdom will take you to better places—and maybe some very interesting ones too!

Michael Voligny serves as vice president for development at HOPE *worldwide* in Wayne, Pennsylvania. He oversees the fund-raising activities of HOPE *worldwide* and is responsible for coordinating relationships with individual donors, corporations, foundations and institutions around the world. Prior to his current position, Michael served as assistant director of East Asia Operations at Harvard University. In close coordination with the offices of the president and provost, he helped to broaden the university's international development activities, particularly in Asia. He came to Harvard in 1989 and held a variety of senior development positions at the Graduate School of Design and the School of Public Health. During his ten years at Harvard, Michael was involved with the planning and implementation of the university's capital campaign that raised more than two billion dollars in five years. Before coming to Harvard, Michael managed architectural practices at the Morris Group, Inc., in Boston, and Lawrence Goldberg & Associates in St. Louis.

A graduate of Washington University in St. Louis, Michael earned his bachelor of arts degree in architecture and archaeology and his master's degree in architectural history. He began to seek the kingdom in the '70s and was baptized into Christ in Boston in 1989. He and his wife, Agnes, have two children: Emma, 3, and Ethan, 1.

14 Money

It Is More Blessed to Give

Michael Voligny

As a professional fund-raiser for the past thirteen years, I have often considered myself a "professional beggar." To my knowledge there are no college degree programs for this profession, even though it represents a $200 billion per year business. Most of my colleagues come from a variety of professional backgrounds and include attorneys, bankers, architects and English literature majors. It is a field that attracts a diverse group of people focused on ensuring that needed financial resources are vigorously and ethically sought and that the intent of the donor is honestly fulfilled. We also serve the ideal of philanthropy and are committed to the preservation and enhancement of volunteerism. "Philanthropy" comes from the Greek word *philanthropos* which means "loving people" or "goodwill to fellowmen." Currently, I serve as vice president for development for HOPE *worldwide*, and my mission as a disciple and as a fund-raiser is to do all I can to help meet the spiritual and material needs of some of the world's most challenged people.

A major part of my training and career as a fund-raiser took place at Harvard University. For most of a decade, I participated in two major campaigns to raise monies to advance the educational mission of the university. As a result of these two campaigns, Harvard's combined endowment has grown today to nearly $19 billion. Throughout these campaigns, I had the opportunity to work with a plethora of wealthy individuals, from those who inherited it to those who made it on their own. A common thread that wove them all together was their love of money. Their love ranged from fanatical to lackadaisical, but it was love nonetheless.

Lessons from the Wealthy

As a frontline fund-raiser at Harvard, I was instrumental in building relationships with prospective donors. This aspect of my profession has always been the most fascinating one to me. It is never an easy task to convince people to give up something that they love—especially for something intangible. As I watched prospective donors contemplate financial gifts, I would often ask myself, "Why is it so hard for people to part with their money, especially for a worthy cause?" I believe that Solomon recognized this issue when he wrote, "Whoever loves money never has money enough; whoever loves wealth is never satisfied with his income" (Ecclesiastes 5:10). However, in most cases, their belief in the institution and their trust in its leadership were instrumental in securing the gifts. Yet, they struggled with each gift, piling one stipulation on top of another, as if they would never let go. As large as these gifts were, rarely were they truly sacrificial on the part of the donor.

Money has always been a powerful force for good or evil. While working at Harvard, I had contact with many families for whom wealth provided extraordinary opportunities: access, independence, freedom and enormous capacity to give back to society. On the other hand, I also saw wealth's poisonous side effects that create greed, dependency and lack of concern for one's fellow man. I often heard terrible stories about intergenerational conflict and sibling rivalries surrounding money issues. These rivalries divided and destroyed families. Paul was right when he wrote that the love of money can bring us many griefs and ultimately draw us away from God (1 Timothy 6:10).

Leaving a Legacy

As disciples, our lives are—or should be—defined and shaped by Jesus. Financial wealth will have corrosive effects on us if this statement is not true about us. Substantial financial wealth, whether earned or inherited, has the capacity to undermine the spirituality of the individual. It is our belief in Jesus that can truly stimulate philanthropy by clearly linking givers to the needs of others. Many of the people I solicit are keenly aware of the power their wealth gives them, but blind to the spiritual responsibilities that come with it. Very rarely do I meet a person who asks the question, "How can I use my financial resources to accomplish God's purposes during my lifetime and beyond?"

In my meetings with prospective donors, I always discuss leaving a philanthropic legacy. In my experience we can leave only two types of legacies: a material one and a spiritual one. And we are going to leave legacies whether we plan to or not. The greatest legacy we can leave is to love people more than money. Jesus, our role model, went to great lengths to identify with and love the poor. He made sure that their basic needs were met, and he showed others—those who were rich—how to relate to them and how to leave a lasting legacy:

> Jesus answered, "If you want to be perfect, go, sell your posses-
> sions and give to the poor, and you will have treasure in heaven.
> Then come, follow me." (Matthew 19:21)

God's Economic Plan for the World

In almost every case, the key to my success as a fund-raiser is to help donors empathize with those in need. I remember a situation with a skeptical donor who traveled with me to a remote part of the world to see mothers dying of AIDS and having to leave their children to a future as orphans. After this experience, she made a major contribution to our medical work in that area. This donor's love for the people she watched suffer had become greater than her love of money. Most of my job revolves around creating opportunities for rich people to develop compassion for those in need. Jesus spent most of his ministry loving and caring for the poor—and teaching his disciples to do the same. His legacy is clear.

Through the years, I have struggled spiritually with the cavernous separation between those of modest means and those who are superrich—the infamous billionaires of the world. This year's *Forbes* "440 Richest People in America" have a combined net worth of almost $1 trillion dollars, which is equal to the combined total income of the bottom half of the world's population. What a staggering statement of the inequitable distribution of wealth in the world today.

Ronald J. Sider's book *Rich Christians in an Age of Hunger* provides an excellent insight into the Biblical view of wealth and God's original economic plan for our world. Based on his book, it is likely that "Christians" represent the single wealthiest economic group of people on earth. If there are needy people in the world, those proclaiming to follow Christ should naturally be the first to meet those needs. Reading Leviticus 25 and Deuteronomy 15 gives us a glimpse into God's desire to see that everyone's needs were met under the old covenant.

> Give generously to him and do so without a grudging heart; then because of this the LORD your God will bless you in all your work and in everything you put your hand to. There will always be poor people in the land. Therefore I command you to be open-handed toward your brothers and toward the poor and needy in your land. (Deuteronomy 15:10-11)

This same spirit is found in the New Testament in a passage like this one that Paul wrote to the church in Corinth.

> Our desire is not that others might be relieved while you are hard pressed, but that there might be equality. At the present time your plenty will supply what they need, so that in turn their plenty will supply what you need. Then there will be equality, as it is written: "He who gathered much did not have too much, and he who gathered little did not have too little." (2 Corinthians 8:13-15)

Clearly, we who follow Jesus must care more about others' needs than we care about our net worth or the size of our portfolios.

A Spiritual Legacy

Philanthropy or caring for the needs of others is a spiritual legacy we can all leave. For those of us who are parents, we know that children will not always do as we say, but they will often do as we do. For example, if we are passionate about meeting the physical needs of others, they probably will be too. Even though my daughter, Emma, is only two years old, my wife and I are already teaching her about orphans and their needs and how we must pray for them and care for them. We hope she will soon understand that there are great spiritual rewards for compassion and generosity: how using our resources to help others is an instrument for happiness because it makes God happy. It is not unusual for my daughter to ask me "Daddy, are you going to help the orphans today?" I want her to understand that money can be an instrument to do good when motivated by true spirituality and a thankful heart.

In our society today, parents need to think seriously about the philanthropic legacy they plan to leave their children. Giving children a sense of value and respect for money and the effort it takes to earn it will help them to understand not only the limited supply of it, but also that it can be easily abused. When parents add a spiritual dimension, by combining this with a Biblical view of God, they will help their children to learn the value of philanthropy and the opportunities it gives to bring glory to God. So much of what comes from the gospel is about philanthropy or the love of our fellow man over the love of self and money. Giving to those in need helps to create a meaningful legacy for you and your family. What kind of legacy do you want to leave—to your family, to society, to the kingdom?

Where Is Your Hope?

> Command those who are rich in this present world not to be arrogant nor to put their hope in wealth, which is so uncertain, but to put their hope in God, who richly provides us with everything for our enjoyment. Command them to do good, to be rich in good deeds, and to be generous and willing to share. In this way they will lay up treasure for themselves as a firm foundation for the coming age, so that they may take hold of the life that is truly life. (1 Timothy 6:17-19)

We are commanded not to put our hope in wealth but "to be rich in good deeds" and generous with our possessions. This will provide us with a lasting philanthropic legacy. Money is a means to an end; our use of it has important spiritual consequences. We must not love money, but what we must love is its ability to help people more.

Here are a few questions to ask yourself if you want to create a lasting philanthropic legacy:

- Have you allowed spiritually minded people to be those who most influence your attitude toward money?
- Are your children developing attitudes toward money that are shaped by spiritual thinking?
- How deep are your convictions about philanthropy or giving to those who have needs?

Ray Humphrey received a bachelor of arts degree, with a concentration in English and philosophy, from Georgetown University. A three-time member of the US national track and field team, he went on to get his juris doctor degree from Georgetown University Law Center.

A previous faculty member at Georgetown and spokesman for the NCAA, Ray moved to Atlanta as part of the 1996 Centennial Olympic Games and as a community liaison for the Make a Wish Foundation. With a legal background and personal development expertise, he has made great contributions to the success of a variety of corporate cultures, including Turner Sports, AT&T, Riverwood International, Magellan Health Services and BellSouth Corporation.

Ray and his wife, Tabatha, are middle-school ministry leaders for the Atlanta Church of Christ, and he is an alumni interviewer for Georgetown University. He is currently the senior program director for HOPE *worldwide* Georgia. His mentoring and tutoring programs serve more than a thousand children annually.

15 Excellence

A Mindset

Ray Humphrey

Excellence is a mindset. I am more convinced of this today than ever before. It is truly a matter of internal pursuit that begins with a fixing of the mind. Visualize with me for a moment that you are striving to reach a goal. Picture yourself actually reaching the ultimate performance level. Can you see yourself there, walking in victory? Will you make it there no matter what happens—regardless of adversity or struggles? This mindset is the cornerstone of excellence:

> Finally, brothers, whatever is true, whatever is noble, whatever is right, whatever is pure, whatever is lovely, whatever is admirable—if anything is excellent or praiseworthy—think about such things. Whatever you have learned or received or heard from me, or seen in me—put it into practice. And the God of peace will be with you. (Philippians 4:8-9)
>
> "Set your minds...." (Colossians 3:2)

I firmly believe in the power of setting my mind. This conviction has become a great asset for me and works as a compass for a greater focus on my long-term goals. It also works as an effective fuel for short-term motivation. The right mindset has always led me to what others would call my "overachievement" in sports, education, business and even my daily walk with God. Setting my mind on the end point in all of these areas was actually the very first step in achieving my goals. With this perspective, I was able to keep a fresh outlook. I saw progress in areas where others saw only pointless routine. I have developed the ability to set my mind on greater goals and have enjoyed the blessings of that exercise.

Spiritual Excellence

In a spiritual sense, excellence for me is not achieving human perfection, but rather, the adherence to a godly standard. This is often expressed as "a wholehearted attempt" and distinguished by the quality of the experience. In its truest form, excellence is never a destination, but a quest. It requires a devotion to the goal that is oblivious to deterrence and impervious to third-party skepticism.

> Not that I have already obtained all this, or have already been made perfect, but I press on to take hold of that for which Christ Jesus took hold of me. Brothers, I do not consider myself yet to have taken hold of it. But one thing I do: Forgetting what is behind and straining toward what is ahead, I press on toward the goal to win the prize for which God has called me heavenward in Christ Jesus. (Philippians 3:12–14)

Experience has taught me that excellence begins with a mindset of faith, which is a decision of trust and wholehearted commitment. Paul writes about this very idea to the brotherhood in Philippi. I totally admire Paul's vision. He sees everything with a divine perspective, with his eyes set firmly on Christ and the spreading of the gospel. Therefore, Paul rejoices and urges his brothers to do likewise. He operates with a belief in a future that has already begun today. He calls us to complete the task with assurance and a guarantee of the vision's fulfillment: "Only let us live up to what we have already attained" (Philippians 3:16).

It is obvious that Paul's mind is set on citizenship in heaven and not the immediate groans and pains of prison—or of any other earthly dwelling. He has a true passion and one defining purpose in life: Christ Jesus. His writings are a call to steadfast adherence to the gospel. Even his arrest and imprisonment are not seen as failures, but rather as triumphs.

I too have learned to keep my focus on the quest. No longer grounded in selfish ambition or blinded by talent, I now remain focused on the realization of a heavenly pursuit. The word of God remains the very center of my daily walk, and with spiritual discipline, I vow to stay the course. I take hold of this everyday as I get up in the morning, put on my sweats, lace up my shoes and head out for my morning run.

An Athletic Standard

What is your standard? We all have standards to contend with in our lives. I now know that most of my own values and principles did not come from within me, but from external sources. Like everyone else, I face external standards of conduct, standards of performance, standards of living, and standards of just about everything else. I have been blessed with various mentors and models upon which to pattern my life and have ultimately reached the following conclusion: in order to reach a true level of excellence, first consider the quality of your standard.

As a high school athlete, I established performance standards that were both arrogant and elusive. "Anything you can do, I can do better!" was my credo, and for a short period of time, this bravado served me well. I had been blessed with a great gift from God. He gave me two strong legs, and my early success in track and field caused me to take this gift for granted. I loved the sport, but I never had to work very hard or concentrate my efforts in order to be successful. Because my talent came with ease, I was confident that God had simply made me exceptional. My overly inflated ego was painfully obvious. This all changed when I left home for college.

As a seventeen-year-old freshman in college, one of the most significant figures in my life was my track coach. Everyone affectionately called him "Coach Gags." He had coached several Olympic athletes and was highly regarded as one of the most elite college coaches in the sport. Gags was a very stout, strong-willed Italian overlord, forever barking expletives and making unreasonable demands on my time—or so I thought.

I will never forget the day when Coach seemed disturbed with the performance of our entire team. He was particularly upset with me. Even though I had yet to lose in competition, he was offended by my indifference on the practice field. He walked up, stood inches from my face and bellowed; "Humphrey, when are you going to put your heart into it and become a runner? Do you want to make it to the top? Well, do you? Can you see where you are going, son?...Think about it!" Then he just walked away and left me standing in silence. I had heard him unleash before, but there was something different in the way that he said those particular words. "Can you see where you are going?...Think about it!" I can still hear him in my head today. I knew exactly what Coach was saying, and it really moved me. I went home that day and wrote his words on an index card. Then I reached into my footlocker and pulled out a picture of the Olympic rings and pinned them and the card to the wall above my bed. Now I would always have something to shoot for, and I vowed to make the most of every day's work.

But there was more; I had a plan. I decided to significantly elevate my personal, private training standards. I would get out of bed before daybreak, put on my sweats, lace up my shoes, and head out for a run at least three times per week. These were my morning runs, and I did them, along with a dozen other daily rituals, in complete privacy every week for the rest of the season.

One of my memorable routines was reserved for Sundays. Sunday was supposed to be our day off from practice, but not for me. I chose to use this day to visit the Metro steps. I was attending school in Washington DC, a city known for its extraordinary underground rail system, which has some of the longest declining escalators in the world. I would set out at 9:00 AM every Sunday during my fall training to do six to eight repetitions up and down the fifty-yard bank of escalators, wearing my headphones and a great, big, puffy twenty-five-pound weighted vest.

Going up the down escalators like this was never an easy task. There were frequently dozens of early morning bystanders and church-folks getting in the way. Several times I had gone home bleeding from a nasty spill. There were also times when the city's finest would kindly escort me to the curbside with a warning. On occasion, I would draw a sizeable crowd of spectators and tourists, gawking at my perceived foolishness. All they saw was the danger, sweat and pain of a fanatic in a space suit, but I would never be deterred. I had my eyes on something greater.

Truth be told, I really hated those morning runs. The mornings were always cold, dark, and the runs would be painful—but I could not forget Coach's words. I had become relentless, not outwardly intense, but inwardly driven and persistently devoted to everything about the sport. I doubt if my teammates ever knew the details of my morning runs, but everyone saw the difference in my demeanor and performance.

All the hard work and sacrifice never really ended for me. I was all about the grind and genuinely fixed on the daily application of effort. This paid great dividends too. I was selected as team captain for all four years of my collegiate eligibility. I also went on to become a six-time All-American, twelve-time conference champion, and four-time team MVP. Before all was said and done, I had qualified for four Olympic Trials and served as director of athlete services for the 1996 Olympic Games.

No, I never did like those morning runs, but I learned to love the pain, because for me, pain meant progress. Every day, every practice and every repetition provided another opportunity to advance. My perspective was simple: I would do whatever it took for as long as required to reach my goals. For the first time in my life, I saw where I wanted to go.

Giving Yourself Fully

I now know that excellence is a wholehearted commitment requiring that you give yourself fully. It is truly about attitude and determination, even amidst the "mundane" details. These details may be considered mundane to others, but they are essential particulars to the one who is driven. In fact, there are no unimportant details for the one who is passionately involved, and in my mind, athletics provides the greatest of metaphors.

I never knew how great things were for me as a track athlete. Since every day was evaluated and measured, the stopwatch and measuring tape were always operating like silent foes, just waiting for me to slacken. I found that I was never really competing head-to-head with another person, but rather, I was constantly pulled forward by a vision. I was well aware that the great pressure of the daily grind would eliminate many contenders, which gave me extra strength to make the daily decisions. These decisions fed my actions and my actions fed my beliefs. I thank God that good was no longer good enough for me. I had learned to set my mind on loftier goals.

The 'Olympic' Experience

"Olympic"—the word itself speaks of monumental significance and is defined in our culture as the pinnacle of performance and achievement. I will never forget the incredibly emotional experience of standing on the infield of the Olympic Stadium as director of athlete services. Track and field was my thing. I had made many US teams before and had more than my share of extraordinary experiences. However, the one defining accomplishment in "amateur" sports is the Olympic games.

I will never forget the opening ceremonies of the 1996 Olympic Games. I can still see the colorful parade of athletes and hear the music. I stood on the infield and looked up at the stadium seats, filled with countless thousands. It was a breathtaking moment. To think that I would get the chance to stand on this field among such royalty was awesome! I had truly come a long way from the small town in up-state New York. It was surreal, and I felt very much out of place as I stood there trembling. I remember the scene as if it were yesterday, and I remember writing how I felt on the back of my Centennial Games program: "A handkerchief on a field reserved for flags."

Taking a Stand

I never won Olympic gold; however, I am more than content with the understanding that I did not toil in vain. I gained something less tangible in nature, yet far greater in value. Having endured the hardships to "make the team," I found that it was not the achievement of my goal, but rather my devotion to the quest that proved to be of greatest import. Now I understand the constant flow of tears in the eyes of the athletes on the award stand.

I finally realize the hidden truth of my experience that would transfer far beyond the athletic experience: I had developed a passion and a commitment to daily growth, the secret to excellence. Unbeknownst to me, from the very moment that I decided to hold fast to the vision, I had already achieved something great. I had taken my stand.

> But the noble man makes noble plans,
>   and by noble deeds he stands. (Isaiah 32:8)

Bill Boyles attended the University of Florida, graduating in 1973 with a degree in accounting. He then attended the University of Florida College of Law, graduating with his law degree in 1976 and his master's of law in taxation in 1978. He has been a shareholder of Gray, Harris & Robinson, PA, in Orlando, where he had been a practicing attorney since 1978. He is rated as an "AV"® attorney by Martindale-Hubbell and has been selected as a Florida Leading Attorney. Also a licensed CPA, he specializes in tax, health-care, corporate, estate-planning and tax-exempt-organization law, with an emphasis on business transactions.

Bill serves as general counsel to Parrish Medical Center, UCF Foundation, Florida Hospital Foundation, HOPE *worldwide*, Excel Alternatives and numerous others. Bill has also handled many corporate mergers and acquisitions. Bill and his wife, Laura, have two sons, Bill Jr. and John.

16 Openness

Letting the Light In

Bill Boyles

When I read my Bible, I am struck by the way men of God open their hearts. Job cries out to God in his afflictions, "I cry out to you, O God, but you do not answer; I stand up, but you merely look at me" (Job 30:20). Job tells God how he feels and about the helplessness and frustration in his heart. He begs God to answer him and God does answer. Job's response is to repent and share his heart of repentance and humility with God.

> "You said, 'Listen now, and I will speak;
> I will question you,
> and you shall answer me.'
> My ears had heard of you
> but now my eyes have seen you.
> Therefore I despise myself
> and repent in dust and ashes." (Job 42:4-6)

The book of Psalms is filled with David pouring out his heart to God in song, begging for God to hear, to rescue, to help and giving praise to God for his victories and bowing before God in repentance. (See Psalm 4, 6, 7, 9, 18, 51.)

Jesus opened his heart daily to his disciples and to his opponents. He was honest and open about what was going on.

> "I am sending you out like sheep among wolves. Therefore be as shrewd as snakes and as innocent as doves." (Matthew 10:16)

> "My soul is overwhelmed with sorrow to the point of death. Stay here and keep watch with me." (Matthew 26:38)

> "O Jerusalem, Jerusalem, you who kill the prophets and stone those sent to you, how often I have longed to gather your

children together, as a hen gathers her chicks under her wings, but you were not willing!" (Luke 13:34)

"Judas, are you betraying the Son of Man with a kiss?" (Luke 22:48)

All these passages show us Jesus' heart—the concern, the compassion, the sorrow, the hurt and the struggle. The revealing of Jesus' heart makes him more real to us as both man and God.

Throughout the New Testament, we see men and women opening their hearts. Peter, Paul, James, Mary, Martha and others shared their thoughts, fears, doubts, victories and defeats. Yet, often in my own life and in the lives of men and women around me, this open sharing is not the norm. Ask yourself: am I an open person? Then ask your spouse, your friends and your children. And listen to their answers.

I want to share with you my journey to becoming a more open person. We each have a choice: either to overcome our fear, open our hearts and grow to be more like Jesus and closer to God or give to in to our fear, keep our thoughts and feelings inside and slowly die spiritually. For most professionals, the latter course is the easier one. Therefore, it is the one that many choose.

Overcoming a Closed Past

As a child, talking about our feelings was not encouraged in my family, and therefore, to me it was not a necessary part of life. Then later I found that for an attorney, expressing or even thinking about your deepest thoughts and concerns is not considered an asset. As a result, I gave little effort to discovering my feelings, thoughts and concerns. Instead, my focus became my list of tasks to accomplish and the analysis necessary to accomplish each one. I was comfortable there. To go outside that realm was scary to me. Consequently, I developed a conditional type of openness, openness about parts of me, but not all of me. Yet to have the relationships I desire with God and others, I discovered that I needed to regularly open my heart.

Like each of you, when I became a disciple of Jesus, I opened my heart to God and to those around me. I revealed dark and hidden secrets that no one had known but God and me. At that time, I was determined to stay open and give my heart fully. My dream as an idealistic college student was to be part of a fellow-ship of disciples of Jesus with whom I could be knit together at the heart. As a young disciple, I often shared the fears, feelings and frustrations that I was aware of in my heart with Sam Laing who discipled me.

When I graduated from law school and moved to Orlando, added responsibility was sadly accompanied by a decrease in my openness. I thought I was open, but those around me knew better. I had allowed the world to define openness for me.

A number of years ago, Reese Neyland and J. P. Tynes sat down with me early one morning for a talk. Reese and I had been in a discipling relationship for many months. He began by saying he knew a lot about me, but did not know me. His statement cut me. Looking back now, I see that what he wanted was my heart—what goes on inside, the self talk, fears and feelings that all of us have—the good, the bad and the ugly. Thus began my quest to identify, understand and reveal what I think and really feel on a daily basis.

A Quest for Openness

God knew that as I grew up, "doing" was highly valued. I was taught that I am defined by what I do, not by my feelings because feelings simply get in the way of doing. Therefore, in my spiritual life I had trained myself to set aside my feelings and act. In fact, my rule was to do what is right and let the feelings follow. While this is a great principle if a disciple is open about his feelings and thoughts, in my life Satan had twisted my thinking, and I ended up burying my feelings. Part of Satan's deception was the fear that if others really knew what I thought, they would not love me or respect me. Thus, to those around me, I became a shallow person. Yet God wanted me to see the unseen, the real me—the thoughts, feelings, fears, joys and happiness deep within my heart (Psalm 51:6, 10)—and to reveal that unseen me to others. Only then could I be molded into the image of Jesus. So I began to pray and search on a regular basis for what I was thinking and feeling.

Several years later, the couple discipling my wife, Laura, and me, Alex and Pree Hull, asked if we could vary our normal practice of having lunch together at a restaurant and meet in their home. As we settled in, Alex opened with, "This is a time for you, Bill." He proceeded to help me see how I was withholding my heart from my wife and holding her back spiritually. The root causes of this were my unwillingness to seek help in our relationship and my lack of openness to Laura's input. Again, in my relationship with my wife, I realized that my focus was on my actions, not on my thoughts and feelings. Therefore when Laura would try to help me and share her thoughts with me, I would be defensive and not listen. She would then feel unloved and unwanted. Through many tears, I repented and opened my heart more and more to input from those around me and especially to Laura.

My relationship with Laura has changed radically since that day. I truly listen to her and her thoughts. If we disagree, we can sit and talk things through without anger or sarcasm. She feels listened to and loved. I can honestly say after nearly twenty-five years of marriage, we are closer and more in love than ever before.

A few years later my family was in crisis. My oldest son, Bill Jr., and I were not getting along at all, and nothing I did helped. (Mostly I stayed angry and hurt.) Counseling was recommended to us, and so off we went. I was thinking and feeling on the one hand, "I don't have a problem" and on the other, "I must really be messed up." After spending time with each one of us, the counselor called me in with my youngest son, John. I was surprised, since I thought the counseling was about my relationship with Bill Jr. He asked John to share his heart with me. As he sobbed, John said, "Dad, I just want to know you!" I cried as I saw how my sin, my lack of sharing and opening my heart, had hurt John. I decided that day to change and open my heart daily to him.

John and I have worked and worked during the last four years to draw closer to each other. The practice of daily giving your heart is hard. It takes a conscious, daily decision. One thing that motivates me is remembering my son's eyes as he looked at me and said, "I just want to know you!" Today, my relationship with John is much deeper. I freely share my heart and thoughts with him, and he does the same with me.

My relationship with my oldest son, Bill Jr., has also radically changed. We have been through a lot together during the past several years. I believe he feels he can honestly talk to me about what is happening in his life, even if he knows it will hurt me or it is not what I want to hear. I am able to share my feelings with him on a heart level. We still often disagree, but we are striving to be closer to each other and build bridges in our relationship. We have made much progress.

A Daily Need for Openness

It was at about the time we went for family counseling that I began a practice which has helped me to open wide my heart. I began keeping a journal. Each day, I begin it with "Today I feel _____!" I made a list of feeling words (happy, sad, excited, scared, frustrated, unsettled, like a failure, etc.) and daily identify what I am feeling. On most days I feel conflicting things. Once I write my feelings down, I can talk about them, pray about them and begin to sort them out. I share these feelings with several friends. In this way, if my feelings are leading me in ungodly directions, I can repent. In any case, when I share my feelings and thoughts, my friends get to know the real me and certainly are in a better position to offer me the help I need.

Throughout the last several years, more and more challenges have come my way from people and circumstances. A common theme runs through them all: be open and open your heart wide. I even participated in a series of secular seminars designed to help people change to become better. The challenge issued to me by the seminar leader and my fellow participants was to "be open-hearted." Over and over again, I see in my life my need to be open.

But God is merciful and he will make this weakness my strength (2 Corinthians 12: 9–10). He has blessed me with many examples of men and women who are radically open. A man who has shown this openness to me is Tom Kuhn, an elder in the

Miami Church. I have known Tom for many years, and one of the many things that I appreciate about him is that he just blurts out what is going on in his heart. As a systems engineer, he too is a very task-oriented, analytical person, yet he fights through and shares his heart. For me, he has become a model to imitate, a model of openness.

Accepting the Challenge

I am convinced that as professionals, each of us must examine how we open our hearts. Do you really say what is going on inside? Do you even know? Or do you project a totally together image? Are you afraid to let others know what is going on inside? God desires each of us, like the Corinthians, to open wide our hearts. Yet, for many of us this is difficult, if not impossible in our own strength. We are driven by a list of things we have to do, not by who we are. Our fear controls us. It is easier to discuss our tasks, rather than our sins and thoughts and feelings. Confession is not second nature; instead, it is nonexistent. Satan loves the darkness. His desire and vision for each of us is to be isolated, alone and separated from God, our families and our brothers and sisters.

Our families and our friends are waiting for each of us to open wide our hearts. The church needs what each of us can give if we will let God work in our lives. Without opening our hearts, he cannot work. Without opening our hearts, our children will scream on the inside, "I just want to know you" and then, frustrated, allow that part of their hearts to die. Without opening our hearts, our wives or husbands will wonder when they will be able to connect and really know us. Without opening our hearts, those who disciple us will wonder, "What is really going on?" Without opening our hearts, those we lead or disciple will wonder why what we say just does not ring true.

If we decide to open our hearts and just walk out in the light (1 John 1:7), God can do amazing things in our lives. With open hearts, our wives, children, disciplers and disciples will know us. With open hearts, we will be more like Jesus. With open hearts, we will be free to truly love those around us and impact them for an eternity. But with openness comes responsibility, a responsibility to be willing to change. Laura often reminds me of that responsibility when, after I have shared my thoughts, attitudes or sins, she simply says, "I appreciate your openness with me. But being open is not the end, it's the beginning because now you know what you need to change." She then encourages me and helps me to change. It is at times like these when I know what Jesus meant in John 8:32 when he said, "Then you will know the truth, and the truth will set you free." Will you take the challenge today to open your heart, know the truth and allow God and others to help you change?

For more help and inspiration, see volume 2 in this series

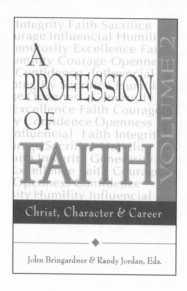

Part 1: Biblical Characters

Zacchaeus	Greg Garcia
Rich Young Man	John Thorne
Aquila and Priscilla	Doug and Ann Deam
Lydia	Cynthia Harris
Alexander	Jeff Tabor
Onesiphorus	Al Baker and James Stein
Felix	Bill Lawton

Part 2: Themes

Attitude	Vivian Rivera-Hanes
Humility	Gerry Fredrick
Integrity	Cecil Wooten
Personal Growth	Ken Lowey
Materialism	Randy Jordan
Success	Sam Holty
Mentoring	C Mack
The Church	John Bringardner

Who Are We?

Discipleship Publications International (DPI) began publishing in 1993. We are a nonprofit Christian publisher affiliated with the International Churches of Christ, committed to publishing and distributing materials that honor God, lift up Jesus Christ and show how his message practically applies to all areas of life. We have a deep conviction that no one changes life like Jesus and that the implementation of his teaching will revolutionize any life, any marriage, any family and any singles household.

Since our beginning, we have published more than 120 titles; plus, we have produced a number of important, spiritual audio products. More than 1.3 million volumes have been printed, and our works have been translated into more than a dozen languages—international is not just a part of our name! Our books are shipped regularly to every inhabited continent.

To see a more detailed description of our works, find us on the World Wide Web at www.dpibooks.org. You can order books by calling 1-888-DPI-BOOK twenty-four hours a day. From outside the US, call 978-670-8840 ext. 227 during Boston-area business hours.

We appreciate the hundreds of comments we have received from readers. We would love to hear from you. Here are other ways to get in touch:

Mail: DPI, 2 Sterling Road, Billerica, Mass. 01862-2595
E-Mail: dpibooks@icoc.org

Find us on the
World Wide Web

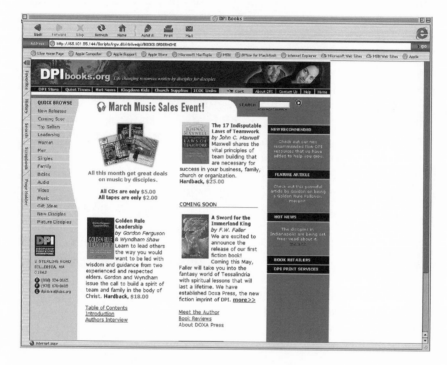

www.dpibooks.org

1-888-DPI-BOOK

Outside the US,
Call 978-670-8840 ext. 227

A
PROFESSION
OF
FAITH